D1548330

Betrayal and Betrayers

BETRAYAL AND BETRAYERS

The Sociology of Treachery

Malin Åkerström

Transaction Publishers
New Brunswick (U.S.A.) and London (U.K.)

Library of Congress Catalog Number: 90-10800
ISBN: 0-88738-358-0
Printed in the United States of America

Library of Congress Cataloging-in-Publication Data

Akerström, Malin.
    Betrayal and betrayers: the sociology of treachery / Malin Akerström.
        p.   cm.
    Includes bibliographical references.
    ISBN: 0-88738-358-0
    1. Trust (Psychology)–Social aspects. 2. Confidence–Social aspects. I. Title.
HM291.A422   1990
303.6–dc20   90-10800
                                                                  CIP

Contents

Acknowledgements

I want to thank Hemisphere Publishing Co. for the permission to reprint articles that appeared in *Deviant Behavior*, 7:1–12, 1986, *Deviant Behavior*, 9:155–167, 1988, and Transaction Inc. for an article that appeared in *Society*, 26, no 2:22–26, 1989.

Carole Gillis has not only helped me to correct my English and to translate quotes from Swedish to English, but also being a classicist discussed illustrations of betrayal themes from mythology. Fabian Persson and Christina McKnight have similarily helped me find such incidents from the past – real and fictional. Kerstin Nyström has typed much of the manuscript. The staff at Transaction provided very helpful editorial assistance. Stina Persson and Sonja Nilsson took care of my children.

Robert M. Emerson gave me early support and encouragement while a guest researcher at the Department in Lund, as did Professor Johan Asplund and the late Professor Vilhelm Aubert. The prompt contract offered by the editor, Irving Louis Horowitz, in response to a question about the idea for the book, certainly served as support.

Funds have been provided by the Scandinavian Research Council for Criminology, Stiftelsen Lars Hiertas minne and Magnus Bergvalls stiftelse.

Preface

The present book attempts to analyze different forms of betrayal. Concrete forms of betrayal or treachery are the trusted diplomat who turns out to be passing on information to the enemy – the spy; the workers who do not join the strike – the scabs; the informer in criminal groups – the snitch; the trusted colleague who suddenly decides to reveal dark secrets from his work – the revealer; those who work with the enemy during conflicts – the collaborators. These are well established social types; but apart from them, we encounter and are quite occupied with betrayal in everyday life. We are careful what we tell the known gossip, children will not play with the tattletale in school; in short, we weigh our words and select the pieces of information that are appropriate to communicate so that we will not ourselves be labeled gossips.

Still, if we possess a secret we must discipline ourselves to keep it. This is the lure of secrets and the "fascination of betrayal." The need for self-discipline is not necessarily because others ask for or demand information but for the sheer attraction of revealing – we are unable not to hint around that we possess valued knowledge. At the same time, social types such as the hero, who did not talk even under torture, or "a person with integrity" from everyday life, are obviously appealing. Thus we may be determined to keep the secret while simultaneously attracted to revealing it. Giving away the secret is sometimes called "betrayal."

This social element – betrayal – is something that catches our imagination. We have all betrayed or been betrayed and we have many words to describe it, an indication of its centrality. Our interest is also mirrored in the masses of fiction, newspaper reporting on spies, informers, etc. The title of Simmel's essay "The Fascination of Betrayal" is to the point.

However this fascination is not shared by other classical social scientists. Nor have I, during the course of my work, come across any modern sociological theorist pondering especially on this problem. This is curious since treachery concerns such basic issues as a group's definition of its vital values, its boundaries, its relation to other collectives and furthermore the individual's relation to the collective. The Norwegian philosopher, Jon Hellesnes, has explored the subject but similarily notes, in his book *Jakta etter svikaren* (*Hunting the Betrayer*), the lack of interest among his colleagues: "Some philosophers have mentioned phenomena like betrayal and searching for betrayers in passing, that is in connection with some other topic. But a philosophy book with such a subject as its main topic is unknown to me. Thus, I am treading virgin territory. This has its disadvantages, and clearly its advantages: you lack a guide, but travel lighter." (1978, 9; my translation)

These missing guidelines have meant that I have written about areas that appealed to and interested me. This book is thus an attempt to explore and illuminate a very basic and general social phenomenon that has been neglected. It is my hope that others will find this field of research as exciting and complex as I do.

Introduction

My initial interest in the sociology of treachery arose while doing a study of violence and threats among inmates in Swedish prisons. (Åkerström, 1985b) Of all the possible sources for conflict or violence among prison inmates (such as failing to pay debts or having committed contemptible crimes such as sex-offenses), those that concerned betrayal seemed to me the most sociologically interesting.

While doing research on the criminal informer, I became more and more interested in the area as a general sociological topic. I caught myself taking notes on conversations I had with friends if gossiping about a third person – was this betrayal or not? I worked with other sociological studies and the issue of betrayal kept popping up – one's relationship to the interviewees as an example.

During this period I had kept on looking for a thematized work on treachery or betrayal. I used the University Library's computer search for key words (betrayer, traitor, snitch, etc.) but ended up with no sociological volume treating the subject *per se* and very little as more specific sociological work, for example, on traitors to the country or alike.

I searched (admittedly unsystematically) the indexes of our classics, our minor classics, and other possible sociological literature. No luck there either.

Perhaps though I had missed some vital work? To make sure, I finally consulted the late Professor Vilhelm Aubert and Professor Johan Asplund, both well-read in the sociological literature and both interested in this type of sociology. They confirmed that to their knowledge no thematized sociological work existed on the topic, and they also encouraged me to continue since they considered the theme as exciting as I did.[1]

The resulting work, this book, is a combination of both the analyses which concern criminal informers only as well as analyses dealing with a wider context and thus more general sociology. For this I have used reports on diverse contexts since my goal has been what Simmel called formal sociology: to find generalities in spite of very different concrete content. The different chapters are meant to stand by themselves, although there are, inevitably a few cross-references.

Sources and Methods

The method and material for this study derives from several sources. The study of criminal informers derived from in-depth interviews with Swedish prisoners. The specifics about methods and sample are described in the Appendix. Apart from this primary material I have conducted some interviews with policemen in conjunction with research on police work conducted by Britta Andersson, a graduate student.

The material is mainly collected from other sources. These include the use of some of my own previous studies. Old field notes and interviews with staff at some women and victim's shelters became especially interesting due to their emphasis on not revealing their "clients" identities.

Other research sources are publications on sociological field work. In these the authors often discuss strategies for shielding their informants' identities, the balancing act of sometimes not revealing sensitive matters while truthfully reporting, and so on. Moreover, social science studies that generally discuss secrecy in various contexts have been used. The criminological and police science literature has obviously been reviewed as it refers to informers. Furthermore, I draw on biographies and autobiographies. These concern whistleblowers, spies, those related to spies, and members of the Resistance during World War II. Historians' and journalists' account of betrayers and their fates after the McCarthy era have also been used.

The illustrations given are often of a dramatic nature even though I believe that one of the features of betrayal is its normality and commonness. (This is also a major reason for its being an important and vital sociological issue.) The advantage with the dramatic is that it is illustrative. Everyday life examples were therefore sometimes exchanged for dramatic ones since the latter were clearer and more distinct. Furthermore in dramatic contexts such as spying, the ordinary is intermingled with the dramatic. Betrayal not only consists of treachery toward the country but experiences of betrayal are often entangled in relations with family and friends. They will suffer the consequences of the traitor's acts, sometimes in practical ways and sometimes by the experience of having been left out. In spite of my choice of illustrations, I hope the reader will be able to draw parallels from the dramatic contexts to more ordinary ones.

Some practical points: in the text I refer to a We that can be betrayed. The capital W in We is used instead of the more heavy, awkward "we."

The material is partly collected from interviews. Much work has been put into translation and finding the right phrases and slang words, but as always in the process of translating them some of the meaning and flavor disappears. This is especially bothersome with the different nuances for all the Swedish euphemisms, pejoratives, and slang words for "betrayer." This is a price willingly paid, however, by gaining the possibility of reaching a wider audience than the publishing in Swedish would permit.

Notes

1. Perhaps there is a growing interest in the field – at least in the restricted area of traitors in the form of spies. Some recent publications point to this. Corrigan (*Theory, Culture & Society*, 1989) has, for example, recently reviewed Cawelti and Rosenberg's *The Spy Story* (University of Chicago, 1987) and Denning's *Cover Stories: Narrative and Ideology in the British Spy Thriller* (Routledge and Kegan, 1987). King has published an article, "Treason and Traitors" (*Society*, July/August 1989), dealing with images of fictionary and real famous spies.

1

Betrayal and Betrayers

Case 1:

Frank Bossard, war time RAF radar officer, civil servant, technical intelligence officer, and finally guiding weapons work in the British Aviation Ministry, supplied photocopies of secret Aviation Ministry files to the Soviet intelligence in return for money.[1]

Case 2:

Eva telling how she disliked the annual office picnic. Every section was supposed to bring its own blanket and food. One was not supposed to join any of the other sections. Even if one, as she did, usually had coffee and lunch with the others, on this occasion it was taboo. Not to stay on one's blanket was treachery, in her own words. (Private conversation)

The above two cases are very different illustrations of how betrayal can be perceived: one is a dramatic, unusual event; the other less dramatic and more common.

Obviously there are differences between the two. Sociologically however I believe it may be fruitful to analyze them as similar social forms – as breaches of trust.[2] Whether these appear as dramatic or not, it is important to acknowledge that treachery constitutes a central human concern. The importance of trust as a basic relationship has been described by Bateson in the following way:

This is what mammals are about. They are concerned with patterns of relationship, with where they stand in love, hate, respect, dependency, trust and similar abstractions vis-à-vis somebody else. This is where it hurts us to be put in the wrong. If we trust and find that that which we have trusted was untrustworthy; or if we distrust, and find that that which we distrusted was in fact trustworthy, we feel *bad*. The pain that human beings and all other mammals can suffer from this type of error is extreme. (Bateson 1977, 470)

Bateson refers to the strong feelings betrayal arouses. Intense sentiments such as indignation, contempt, revenge, and so on are not reserved for those directly involved. Furthermore they can continue long after the crime took place. Dante is a case in point: in his lusty description of hell in *Divina Commedia* he places the archetypal traitors Brutus and Judas Iskariot in the ninth and worst circle where they are lowered to eternal ice and chewed into small pieces by Lucifer's three maws.

What, then, is this phenomenon that engages us so intensively? Betrayal is easily understood intuitively. Making a more stringent definition is not so easy. I will not suggest a comprehensive definition but I will problematize the concept, and in that process point out some characteristics of that which we experience as betrayal.

Looking for material in the literature on treachery I found mostly characters such as traitors to a country or police informers. Sociologically the subject appears to be much more open for generalities. We also talk about scabs, snitches, deserters, and defectors as social types who betray.[3] My first point of departure therefore is to discuss betrayal as generally as possible, in the Simmelean tradition of formal sociology. This implies a search for different contexts and types of betrayal where discovered similarities and differences are not attributed to the concrete content. My second point of departure is that betraying is a common rather than uncommon feature of social life. Most of us have experienced betrayal such as a child discovering our friend preferred to play with someone else and onward. We have betrayed or been betrayed – at least as fleeting suspicions. My third point of departure is that the breach of trust involved is an overstepping of a We-boundary – the We consisting of relations ranging from a pair of friends to a nation.

Secrets as Creators of Social Bonds

Why are secrets and confidences exchanged when the risk of betrayal exists and possible betrayal can be so painful and/or dangerous? While acknowledging the complexity of this issue one may concentrate on the purely social motives. Simmel, who has written about secrets and secrecy, has emphasized the bonds created by them. According to him secrecy is one of the "great social phenomena" peculiar to man and one of his greatest achievements, giving rise to a parallel world enlarging life. Without secrets many aspects of social life would be impossible. (1964,

330) Furthermore, secrets make for a division of those in the know and those not in the know: a We/Them dichotomy is created. Confidences bind the confiders to each other. Societies and groups are created by, and live off, their secrecy.

Aubert used Simmel's analysis when he wrote about his experiences from the Resistance in Norway during World War II. Even in dangerous contexts there is a need for sharing secrets because of the social bonds they create. The Resistance's preference for the organization being led from Norway rather than by those in exile supervising individual local agents not known to each other was perhaps caused by such considerations rather than by the stated arguments, which had a more "rational" character.[4]

> There may have been a feeling that the coldly efficient system of individual agents, isolated from each other, would lead to further deprivations. The possible loss of intimacy and friendship, which existed within the organization and which sustained morale, constituted a latent threat. To be isolated with important and dangerous secrets constitutes a threat to personality, while the sharing of secrets, although dangerous, creates bonds of intimacy. (Aubert 1965, 305)

This quotation illustrates that the dramatic and common everyday life betrayal may not necessarily be different after all. In one and the same context they may be intermingled. One also finds an illustration of the social bonds produced as a result of sharing secrets. In this example they were produced by the sharing in itself (obviously accentuated tremendously by the background of danger).

In other circumstances social bonds may be created by exclusive sharing; that is, leaving someone out by creating We's in a larger We. Goffman has written about collusion, which can be created through such sharing. Collusion need not include direct secrets but rather the sharing of experiences, opinions, and so on that the others in the group are excluded from but that may well involve them. Betrayal in this form seems to be a social necessity in that we use it to indicate the importance or specialness two people or a few members of a group feel toward each other:[5]

> Collusion is a normal and no doubt desirable part of social life . . . it is probably impossible for interaction to continue among three persons for any length of time without collusion occurring, for the tacit betrayal of the third person is one of the main ways in which two persons

express the specialness of their own relation to each other. (Goffman 1972, 340)

Betrayal as Not Honoring the We

Information – not necessarily in the form of secrets but particular information having a special value to a number of people – creates a distinctive form of relation. This is a We. Its members may hold alternative interpretations of the shared information but only they (as opposed to the world around them) know the nuances, meanings, and possibilities of interpretations of that information. The symbol of a flag will mean something more, whether you like it or not, through the eyes of a citizen than through the eyes of a foreigner.

The boundaries around the We are given by shared background and knowledge.   Once these We's are formed, however, they are the determinants of what ought to be shared with outsiders. This is evident when some information is declared secret by the We in principle – not because the revelation would hurt anyone.[6]

The size of the We may differ and its members may be more or less intimate. Some groupings constitute natural We's, such as the family, where we cannot escape common experiences and are given a common background; or the inhabitants of a We may not necessarily know each other. In this sense, We's are not only a pair or a group but may be a nation, a religion, a common people, or a class. Furthermore one may be a member of many We's simultaneously. The propensity of betrayal due to the participation in many different We's holding different, and sometimes opposing, values is characteristic of modern societies.[7] Treachery is thus inherent in the process of socialization:

. . . the problem of *which* "self" is being betrayed at any particular moment, a problem posited as soon as identification with different significant others includes different generalized others. The child is betraying his parents as he prepares for the mysteries and his nurse as he trains for knighthood, just as he betrays his peer group by being a "square" young scholar and his parents by stealing an automobile, with each betrayal concomitant with "treason to himself" in so far as he has identified with the two discrepant worlds. (Berger and Luckmann 1972, 190)

Furthermore We's are not stable entities. They vary for example according to who constitutes Them. Take a place of work. It often consists of competing We's, who will form Them's in relation to each other.   Threatened by an outside enemy, these We's will form one betrayable, unified We.

Betrayal occurs when you in one way or another overstep the boundaries of a We.   In some situations the boundaries become more important and overstepping them more serious (for example,   times of conflict or when individuals or groups have invested a lot in their secrecy).

Forms of Betrayal

Leaving the discussion of the concept as such, one may go on to explore which forms treachery takes and how it is experienced more concretely. The first that comes to mind is that of something being told. Judas, the archetypal traitor, "told." But telling is not the only act that constitutes betrayal – not telling may be an act of betrayal as well. Other actions or lack of actions may also be treacherous.   "Scabs" are, for example, definitely considered as traitors to those on strike.

The breaching of the We's boundaries may analytically be categorized in several ways. Apart from the examples given above, someone may reveal too much in the sense of showing outsiders that which should be hidden by opening the door and letting the outsiders look in in a way that is not considered proper. One may fail to use the defense strategies or face-saving techniques that are expected to protect the team or any of its members from embarrassment. (Goffman 1959) Moreover, one may act in a way that will hurt the We and that is perceived as betrayal. Some such acts, if done secretly, are those labeled "stabs in the back." Leaving the We, thus denying its value, may constitute the most final of betrayals. Betrayal of this sort includes deserting, defecting, or refraining from joining the fight in a conflict.

Below, I have chosen to discuss betrayal in the forms of "telling" versus "leaving." They are quite different forms of behavior; but in this context, sociologically, they have the same meaning. Obviously not all telling and leaving are associated with betrayal. The conditions when labeled as such will be explored. It should be added that both telling and leaving can be present in any one betrayal as when someone decides to inform because he wants to leave the group and informing thus becomes a sign of his commitment to another group.

Telling

Betraying by telling may take several forms. For example, it might be the telling of something we consider secret or deem sacred. Even though the information divulged might be neither secret nor sacred from the point of view of the teller, the receiver/hearer may betray the secret due to the nature of the information received. Such a situation can occur when the betrayed does not realize that his or her behavior might be judged as a misdoing and thus makes no attempt to hide it.

The social welfare organizations may qualify as betrayers in this sense, as for example when they have certain standards that their clients do not know about beforehand. If you turn to them with trust and believe that you form a We with them, expecting help but getting detrimental results, you are apt to feel betrayed. One example of this was given in a study of battered women. (Schillinger 1988) One of the interviewed women had called the police after a former boyfriend broke into her mobile home and beat her and her youngsters. The welfare case worker who was called in had the children put in foster homes. After this the battered woman's anger was directed at the authorities instead of the former boyfriend. Apart from the fact that the loss of the children probably was more painful than the battering, she might also feel betrayed because she believed that in this case she was a "deserving victim" entitled to help and that she would form a We with the police and the social worker against the boyfriend. Instead, the authorities turned against her by taking her children away from her. Schillinger makes the general comment:

> What surprised me, however, was that in most instances the main thrust of their considerable anger was directed not at the battering mate, but at what was perceived to be the equally brutal and patriarchal welfare bureaucracy. (Schillinger 1988, 477)

Telling about that which we call secrets may involve everything from breaking confidences of friends to revealing religious rites. Betrayal among friends, for example, seems to be closely associated with the discovery that sensitive information cannot be passed on. In a study of high school students it is said:

> The most prominent feature of friendship is to be found in connection with "trust." . . . For our students, "trust" meant being able to *talk* and knowing in turn the other would *not talk* – behind your back. He could receive confidences and keep them. Indeed the break-up of friendship, as distinct from drifting apart, involved precisely the feeling the other had let one down. (Naegele 1958, 243)

Divulged secrets are not the only things that can hurt or injure the exposed party. Some of the experiences we share with another are invested with a kind of sacredness. One wants to keep the specialness in one's relations, and to cover up some of the members' practices and thoughts that are not deemed appropriate for the outside world. Social scientists sometimes come close to seeing themselves or being seen by others as "spies" and when reporting about their material as "informers." Their special problem is that they have gained entrance to a We, and then they have discussed the people they studied without the proper deference which includes hiding and shielding that which is not to be shared with outsiders. They can thus be seen as having profaned the sacredness of the We built on common information and background. It is this that infuriates people.

> The hatred occasionally visited upon the debunking historian is visited almost daily upon the person who reports on the behavior of people he has lived among; and it is not so much the writing of the report, as the very act of thinking in such objective terms that disturbs the people observed. It is a violation of apparently shared secrets and sentiments. (Hughes 1960, xiv)

As it is used here sacred obviously does not have to be connected with traditional religious use. It is used in the Durkheimian sociological connotation implying that humans themselves are viewed as sacred. Parts of our private life are therefore sacred symbols of a We. As to the latter, a good illustration has been provided in an analysis of women involved in extra marital affairs. (Richardson 1988) We all show our membership in a We through different social confirmations. When it is impossible to do this through external validation, signs of belongingness may be invested in things or rituals. All the women in Richardson's study had such ways of "marking We": private language, jokes, anniversaries, phone codes. Even time slots could acquire this quality – one woman told how she and her lover wrote to each other at the same time every day "like we were really together." Some had shared possessions. These objects could take on a semi sacred quality:

> Another woman, after a long preparatory statement, entered her bedroom and positioned herself in front of a bulletin board which held a dried bouquet, a Valentine's Day Card, movie ticket stubs, and some postcards. A period of silent viewing followed. Later, she said, the board was strategically placed "so I can see it just before I turn off my night-light." (Richardson 1988, 215)

The objects so invested with sacredness were not hidden so they were not secret in that sense, but their symbolic meaning was secret. As I see it, the above is illustrative of how a betrayal of the sacred in everyday life could occur. For example, if that woman overheard her lover cynically speaking of these objects, it might destroy the We.

A more obvious betrayal of the sacred occurs when religious beliefs, traditions, or rituals are profaned by revealing them to the uninitiated. This is probably most pronounced when the revelation concern closed or secret societies or tribes. When outsiders gain access to the sacred by identifying with and being accepted by the in-group and then must simultaneously reveal information due to their job or task, I imagine quite a lot of consciences are probed. Journalists or social scientists probably wrestle with this from time to time. Sometimes one decides to honor the We when one judges revelation to be harmful. One example of this concerned revelations from the Australian aboriginal society:

> . . . in some cases the most cherished values and beliefs of the group may be threatened by publication, a fact recognized by anthropologists in the case of some ritual practices, where publication has been managed to avoid, for example, revelations destructive to the traditions of Australian aboriginal society. (Bulmer 1980, 61)

In other cases it has been the members themselves who have exposed the We in an unacceptable manner. Among some American Indians, for example, there seems to be an ongoing debate between those who have openly described their medical practices and those who believe that this is irreverent to their spiritual heritage. Some, called "pink shamans," have created new tribes where both whites and Indians are included. Indian leaders in the "Elders Circle" have reacted to these pink shamans and have stated:

> We therefore want to warn people about these individuals who travel around and play with the spiritual needs and lack of knowledge found in our non-Indian brothers and sisters. The value of these individuals' teaching and ceremonies is negligible, perhaps even worthless, and harmful for those who believe these false "words of truth." (Törnlund. *Sydsvenska Dagbladet* /Swedish daily/ April 7, 1988, p.4)

And they question their belongingness – are they, as Indians, of the pure We? "Which nation do they represent? Which clan and tribe do they belong to? Who teaches them and where?" (Törnlund. Ibid.)

In this connection it might be important to note that secrets not only may protect an inner core in a group and differentiate between We and Them, but they also have a value of its own. The mere fact that something is secret increases its value, and the loss of secrecy may lead to a loss of sacredness. Secrecy gives mystique and excitement; and by revealing the rites of any group (say the Masonic Order, to use another example), their value would decrease and simply appear banal. As Simmel has noted:

> From secrecy, which shades all that is profound and significant, grows the typical error according to which everything mysterious is something important and essential. Before the unknown, man's natural impulse to idealize and his natural fearfulness cooperate toward the same goal: to intensify the unknown through imagination, and to pay attention to it with an emphasis that is not usually accorded to patent reality. (1964, 332)

Leaving

That leaving the group can be defined as betrayal is evident in that some deserters are labeled as betrayers. Not only deserters in war but deserters from many religious sects are cases in point. In exploring the conditions when leaving is associated with betrayal, it might be useful to compare some quite different contexts.

Whether true or false, the theme of deserters being punished in certain Mafia[8] or other tight-knit criminal groups is evident in popular culture. Ed McBain, for example, uses the theme when describing how someone who gets caught up in a closely knit, violent youth gang finds there is no way out. In one scene, he lets the leader warn the doubter:

> I also told Johnny that there was no such *thing* as quitting the clique, that if he refused to go up against the Scarlets tomorrow night, why then, I would consider him a deserter and he might just as well move out of the country because he could never so much as set foot on Rebel turf again without having to pay the full penalty. (1975, 141–142)

Another example involves quite a different group: the Secret Apostles, an exclusive student club at Cambridge to which you could not apply but had to be chosen. Anthony Blunt, Guy Burgess, Maynard Keynes, and Ludwig Wittgenstein, to name a few, have been members. The group hailed the values of the intellect, love, esthetic experiences, states of mind, contemplation, communion. Even though there was no overt, drastic punishments by the group for leaving, leaving was surely seen as betrayal according to the following description of the reaction to Wittgenstein's change of life:

In 1919 he decided to abandon philosophy; he gave his money to relatives and announced that he intended to lead a simple, ascetic life. He worked as a schoolteacher, then tried to make his living as an architect and finally became a gardener in a convent. His admirers insisted that he was wasting his unique talents and, in 1929, he returned to Cambridge. But the Apostles made their displeasure clear. He had abandoned the life of the mind and in doing that had rejected everything the society held precious. At their meeting in Keynes's rooms on 20 April 1929 the Apostles generously decided to forgive him. The meeting decided to "absolve him from his excommunication." (Penrose and Freeman 1987, 67)

In the first case of the violent youth gang, there were instrumental reasons for punishing the deserter – he might snitch. Here, however, no such fears apply. It is a case of a purely moral, value-based condemnation of leaving. The same interpretation of values being abandoned may hold for the denunciation of political refugees who do not return to their native country when a return is made possible. According to a study of Latin Americans who were granted political asylum in Sweden, those who stayed on after they were ultimately able to return are considered betrayers since returning is a moral or political duty. (Lundberg 1989, 163) In this way, they too can be said to have left the group.

There are also leavings in everyday life that may be experienced as betrayals. One illustration is the example given in the beginning of this chapter of the woman who had to stay on her blanket at the picnic for fear of being viewed as a traitor. Comings and goings, whom one talks to or stays with, are furthermore a general way of "marking We." Others comment on who sits with whom at parties, work places, etc.; and if it is out of the ordinary pattern, it is noticed. In Wieder's (1974) study of a halfway house for addicts, this tendency is clearly described. The author was even able to make drawings of different configurations in the dining room – some associations are clearly accepted whereas others are forbidden. Associating with Them – the staff – was not done. Since the researcher himself was also considered as one of Them, he had difficulties in getting to talk to the residents (former addicts); they often left as soon as he got close, sat down beside them, etc., since they did not want to be "grouped" with him in the dining room, in a bar, or wherever they would be seen by other residents.

As noted, leaving may be denounced for instrumental or practical reasons such as fear that the leaver will disclose something; but the basic mechanism seems to be social: interpreting the leaving as a rejection of the values of the We. Illustrations of this are the many situations where leaving is not associated with betrayal. Valued members may leave a work unit for a better position without this being considered a betrayal but rather a "fact of life"; their old colleagues may simply wish them good luck. Leaving a group is evidently not sufficient reason to be considered a traitor, nor is it enough when the leaving is perceived as harmful (as when a valuable colleague leaves).

Intensifying and Mitigating Influences

Some illustrations have been given of when behavior is seen as betrayal. One should recognize however that experiences of betrayal and the punishment of betrayal vary since there are forces that influence its strength one way or the other – some intensify and others mitigate. As betrayal is the breach of trust in the sense of broken expectations from those in the We, an intensifying element is when the betrayer's behavior catches us by surprise. If we are not surprised, his or her acts might still qualify as treacherous but we would not be as upset by them as we might have been. If we are not surprised at all, we have probably begun to doubt the betrayer's membership in the We and the act might not even be considered a betrayal.

In some contexts betrayal is expected whereas in others it is almost unimaginable. Such betrayals may take on a symbolic value. Bateson (1977), for example, believes that not honoring the Treaty of Versailles had a significant effect on modern history so that distrust of the golden rule of accepting agreements was spread.[9] He believes that the basic rule of how to play the game was betrayed (and then changed) after the Treaty. Not honoring treaties or deals has been called "betrayals of the enemy" (Hellesnes 1978, 75–77), but may be seen as violations of a temporary We: peacemakers representing large groups, making promises on their behalf, sacrificing and compromising and then having all that is put on the line cut off. Whatever the interpretation, Bateson is probably right in stating: "Men have felt for centuries that treachery in a truce or peace-making is worse than trickery in battle." (Bateson 1977, 475)

The boundaries around the We may be more or less sharp and well-guarded, and some contexts and situations accentuate them. In times of conflict, the boundaries obviously are more tightly drawn than at other times. Moszkiewiez (1987) has described how it was made clear to her that once she decided to join the Belgian Resistance during World War II, there was no way back – no one was allowed to leave. Such totalitarian demands are not exclusive for groups in open conflict. Some states also apply definitions of leaving as betraying as was seen, for example, in most Eastern European countries, where merely applying for an exit or emigration permit used to constitute treachery. Sharper boundaries are furthermore found around groups or "greedy institutions" (Coser 1974), which have near-total or total demands on their members as some political or religious sects.[10] One of the elements in the accentuation of the boundary thus depends on a stronger We/Them dichotomy than usual resulting from special characteristics of the group or of the situation.

Another element that influences the intensifying versus the mitigating definition of treachery is the consequences it causes. During or after a conflict, where members in a We have invested and paid a lot, punishment will be heavy and acts normally not considered treacherous will be defined as such. Lottman (1986) has described how reactions varied in intensity from 1944 onward during the French purge of those who had collaborated with the enemy.[11] In the beginning of the purge fresh memories of suffering caused feelings to run high. Some of the resistance leaders even tried to hinder reactions they saw as excessive. Yves Farge, for example:

> . . . complained that some people wished to jail anyone connected in any way with the Vichy regime. But the point was to punish real traitors . . . he offered his listeners "some principles of elementary honesty": Wrong opinions are never punishable. . . . The purge must have limits, both in time and in its very concept. Otherwise, "a pure man always finds a purer man to purify him." (Lottman 1986, 105)[12]

Treachery in itself is furthermore judged differently according to how the actor and the motives attributed to him are seen. A dramatic case can serve as an illustration: those traitors being reprieved and those not reprieved but sentenced to death. In France after World War II, only de Gaulle could save a collaborator from the firing squad after a Court of Justice sentenced him to death. How did he decide? " . . . he commuted 1,303 death sentences, notably all of the women, most minors, and most defendants who had acted under orders and while risking their own life. The 768 rejected appeals concerned persons who de Gaulle felt had acted personally, spontaneously, to kill Frenchmen or serve the enemy." (Lottman 1986, 157) His arguments can be said to be based on "intent." Those acting under pressure or taking orders were less to blame than those acting personally and spontaneously. Furthermore, while women might have been pardoned for chevalier reasons, minors (and perhaps also women) in our culture are considered less determined actors than grown-up men.

The morals of individuals always seem to be emphasized when betrayal is discussed. This is due, I believe, to the fact that it is coupled with intent. In this aspect of human affairs we do not see people as marionettes, simply doing things by routine, unreflectingly. We may say about someone who betrays that "he could not help himself." By this, we would not mean that he did it for deterministic reasons but because he could not bear the pressure he was put under. In dangerous situations, people may thus put the issue of whether they would betray their friends or not under torture as "the ultimate moral test." (Aubert 1965, 295) Furthermore, in more ordinary contexts I believe we also judge the conduct of others in regard to intent; for example, whether someone "slipped" or whether he or she revealed something maliciously. Slips of course are more forgivable.[13] The emphasis on morals and the belief in the possibility of choice explains why children or senile persons are not called betrayers by "wise grown-ups," even if they tell or do things that would earn others the title. Even if they belong to the group, in this respect they do not belong to the We in terms of being able to protect the shared information.

An interesting case where several intensifying and mitigating factors seem to be involved is the breakup of marital and friendship We's. Leaving a marital We is institutionalized in the form of "a divorce." This can be compared with friendships where one may sever the relationship without openly stating the reasons and with no rituals attached to the leaving. According to Suttles (1970, 97) this is one of the constituting cultural features of friendship. This feature may give a special form of painfulness, since one never knows for sure what happened. From a book on middle-class women's friendship:

> I can't put it into words because it was so intangible, but I could just feel she was pulling away. We didn't exactly have a falling-out, but it sort of ended. It was so painful to go through because I never really knew why it was happening. (Gouldner and Symons Strong 1987, 134)

In both marriage and friendships there are accepted reasons (vocabularies of motives) for leaving, such as "we drifted apart" which can mitigate the sense of betrayal. Another factor concerning love that explains and thereby mitigates a leaving is its special vocabulary. At least there are sayings underlining our belief in the force of romantic love such as "One cannot resist love," "It was beyond his control," one "falls" (irresistibly) in love, and so on, thus perhaps excusing those who leave a relation for this reason.

Competing We's

In some cultures, friendship is held up and contrasted with love to the advantage of friendship. This means that when the two are compared, greater demands are put on the friends' abilities to discipline themselves regarding the "force of love." It may therefore be the friend rather than the lover who is labeled betrayer. In *Kitchen-Table Society*, an ethnographic analysis of Norwegian, suburban, mostly working-class young women, there is a passage about how a woman has taken a man to her house, someone which her friend, Sissel, has a steady relationship with: "The day after this incident Sissel said that she was much more crushed by the fact that a woman friend could do such a thing to her, than by what Benny [her former husband] did to her by falling in love with another woman." (Gullestad 1984, 251) It may be noted that the lover was not even commented upon.

Sometimes love relations are said to compete with friendship, with friendship winning because it is seen as the more basic and durable of the two. In Whyte's classic *Street Corner Society* an illustration of this is given. One of the corner boys, Frank, feels betrayed by his long-time friend, Alec. The latter has begun to hang around with another young man in the gang, Joe, since Joe has access to a car with which they can take girls out for dates. Frank feels left out and articulates his feelings as follows:

> Let them go out with the girls. They've pulled a few fast ones. They say they're going to do a certain thing, and then you find them with the girls. They've done things that I would never do. . . . It's hard enough to make a friend. A girl you can meet any time. . . . It takes years to make a real friend. (1973, 29)

The same theme, but tied to a classic triangle constellation (unfaithfulness with someone connected to you already[14]), is presented and warned for in different popularized versions, as in a song made known by the singer-guitarist Ry Cooder, where the "I" has had an affair with his best friend's girl, even though: "Me and Frank have been friends for so long and our friendship is really strong. . . ." So he breaks up with the girl by telling her: The love of a friend and the love of a girl are two things you can't compare. . . . Go on home, girl, You've gotta go home now."[15] The general reason for issuing warnings concerning such relationships is that they can destroy We's - probably those consisting of the most important significant others - while simultaneously containing available and sometimes attractive options.

Sometimes the demands for loyalty from the different We's are mutually exclusive. In such situations, where choices of loyalty have to be made, the boundaries of the We become especially pronounced and visible. Many betrayal-situations actually seem to be inevitable for this reason. In modern life where we are members of several often competing social circles, this must be a common dilemma. Divorces, for example, place friends, not to mention children, in situations of divided loyalties, choices, and maneuverings. Among the criminals I have interviewed, choices of loyalties were at times a vital issue (see chap. 6).

A context where the dilemma of loyalty is often dramatically shown is that of spying. Therefore I will use it as an illustration. The propensity for a dilemma depends on one's commitment: is one of the We's especially important? For some, the issue seems unproblematic. Kim Philby, the famous English spy, stated when asked by his wife what was most important, the Communist party or her and their children: "The Party, of course." (Philby, E. 1968, 101) For others the opposite choice is the obviously correct one. The English author E. M. Forster, who, like Philby, once belonged to the Apostles at Cambridge, took his stand for the closest relations: "If I had to choose between betraying my country and betraying my friend, I hope I should have the guts to betray my country." (Forster 1972, 66)

In most such cases involving a larger We in competition with a natural We, the choice for most people is probably more complicated. One such drastic dilemma involves pointing the finger at a relative involved in spying. The American "spy family," the Walkers, was caught when the wife reported her husband. In a book about the family (Blum 1987), it seems uncertain whether she would have reported him if she had known her son was involved as well. Barbara wrote: "God, I hurt. Do you know what it's like to live everyday knowing the decision I have made has done this to my son?"[16] In other examples of spying one finds illustrations of relatives experiencing betrayals. The most drastic choice probably occurs when, if caught, one decides whether to stay or leave the country. A Swedish Army officer, Stig Bergling, escaped after being imprisoned for spying. His mother was subsequently interviewed by the evening papers:

> She has cried many times for her son and his escape. And she feels betrayed. "But it is not only Stig who has betrayed, his wife is guilty as well. I can't understand her doing this and abandoning her children." (*Expressen*/Swedish daily/ April 4, 1988. p. 9; my translation)

The mere fact that one has kept vital parts of one's life secret from those who expect to know can be interpreted as betrayal both by those who keep the secrets and by those who are left out. An example of the latter was the fact that the former Norwegian diplomat Arne Treholt's friends were reported to have felt betrayed by him – not for being a spy, which they doubted he was, but for not having told them about his actions.[17] (Aubert, private conversation) Those who are compelled to conceal important parts of their lives may accept this but still consider it a burden. An example can be seen in a description of the English spy Anthony Blunt's experiences when he had to deceive old friends: "He felt pain for deceiving Tess Rothschild, and other close friends like Dick White and Guy Liddell . . . but it was the pain of what had to be done, rather than the pain of what might have been avoided." (Penrose and Freeman 1987, 225)

Symmetry in Betrayal Relations?

A mental picture of treachery might be triangular – a teller, a told on, and a told to. Furthermore, if the betrayal is discovered, these three parties will agree to the definition of treachery. The constellations, however, may not be so straightforward. Betrayal is not necessarily tripartite. A couple may feel that they betray each other – not to or with someone else. For example, they may have certain expectations of each other that they do not fulfill. Furthermore, one often pictures the actors as one being a victim and the other as being a "wrongdoer." The roles, however, often appear more complex. In a study by Warren (1986) of women mental patients, it is evident that in many cases both they and their spouses saw both themselves and their partners as betrayers. The men felt like betrayers because they had helped commit their wives, while at the same time they felt that their wives had betrayed them by becoming ill. The women no longer took care of the household or the children; their husbands were forced to take over. Their experiences were mirrored by the women, who felt they had let their husbands down while sometimes blaming them for their being in the hospital.

In the cases above the partners agreed to the definition of the betrayals involved. In other cases an asymmetry in relation to whether an act is seen as a betrayal or not, exists. In some cases, one party may feel betrayed while the other does not think that he committed a betrayal. Those working in occupations where one is both supposed to care and control, such as social workers, are apt to be considered treacherous at times even if their actions are well-meaning. The opposite may also occur, of course. In the literature on "burn-out" one of the elements that is included is social workers', or others', experience of being betrayed by their clients.[18] Many of those clients would perhaps describe themselves as "smarties" rather than as betrayers; that is, beating the system rather than breaching the trust of an individual. At other times the betrayed may not feel betrayed, if not informed of the betrayal by others. Those others may help influence the definition of a situation into being a betrayal, and the victim may then define an act as "Ah, that's how it was."

Treachery?

Treachery is often associated with a question mark; that is, recurrent questions of whether an act is a betrayal or whether someone is really a betrayer. The act is different from, for example, stealing as (King 1989) has pointed out. In that case all agree on the theft; the issue is who did it. Furthermore, the role of the betrayer is different from that of, say, being a teacher – either you are, or you are not. The act of betrayal and the role of the betrayer, on the other hand, is thoroughly based in moral evaluations. Whether the act and actors will be defined as treacherous depend on who is defining and on more general values – that may change over time.

Evaluations may change as time makes us reread behavior or actions from the past. On the everyday level take, for example, a child who feels betrayed by his parents for teaming up with the doctor for a painful treatment, but who later realizes that this was for his own good. On a larger scale, that which was seen as a "sell-out" in a negotiation was really the only realistic alternative to accept.

The perspectives applied are also important in that they create different definitions. When choices of loyalty have to be made as to whom to let down, those on the top will see the behavior of the person in question differently from those being let down. Sometimes different perspectives may create such strong social typings that a betrayer in one group may be equivalent to a hero in another. The Norwegian author Rieber-Mohn (1969) not only noted the problem, but has devoted a whole book to the moral definitions and dilemmas concerning the label. The title of his book is consequently *Forraedere*? which means *Traitors*? He wants to nuance the concept and points out that traitors to a country have often been those who have challenged the government, the state, or the community. Some of those called traitors may well be heroes to challengers of the establishment. He questions the image of well-known traitors by exemplifying with some possible heroes, but also includes for example, Pétain and Quisling, and examines their motives to see whether they were perhaps pawns rather than simple evil betrayers. Another Norwegian, the philosopher Hellesnes (1978), discusses an article by his fellow countryman, Bjorneboe (1971), who goes further than Rieber-Mohn. Bjorneboe discusses betrayers as rebels and gives Socrates and Jesus as examples of men who questioned the very thoughts their collectives rested upon. Hellesnes points out that he deals with a special type of treachery.[19] He means that Bjorneboe's discussion centers around those who defy the elite. Betrayers as Judas are left out. Hellesnes further points out that considering the betrayer as one who rebels is an expression of the belief in the autonomous man against the collective, which leaves little room for viewing man, when he acts as an individual, as a societal product. In referring to this discussion of conditions when setting labels on betrayal, I have not wished to enter into the debate but simply to illustrate that the issue is far from black and white.[20]

Another complication lies in the definition of the We. Who "really" belongs? Individuals thought to be part of the We can quickly be redefined as being out. If they turn out not to belong, their acts may not be judged as treachery. We feel fooled rather than betrayed. A drastic illustration of this is given, I believe, in the reaction of a member of the Resistance when captured by the Nazi officer pretending to be in the Resistance. His comment was: "My congratulations, mon Colonel. You played your game well." (Cookridge 1966, 180) Thus, he reinterpreted the situation and congratulated the enemy for winning, rather than accusing the colonel of betrayal.[21] Although the comment sounds a bit like a movie cliché, the feeling behind it may be representative. Discovering that someone is not, after all, one of "us" may make us angry with him or upset that we were fooled, and so on, but perhaps not betrayed.[22] A similar illustration of such distinctions is given in *Spycatcher*. The British Secret Service agents are reported to have commented on a planned arrest of a KGB-spy, Lonsdale, who had assumed a Canadian identity: "It's not as if he's a traitor . . . not like Houghton. He's just doing his job like us." (Wright 1987, 136). Lonsdale was a Russian, thus not in the We, while Houghton originated from the We (the KGB had recruited him through extortion).

These distinctions can also be used by the betrayer. Kim Philby can be said to have defended himself against the label of traitor in this manner. He declared that he had never belonged to the West but had always been a communist and was therefore not a traitor. In his own words: ". . . to betray one first has to belong. . ." (Pincher 1987, 28; Rieber-Mohn 1969, 99)

Betrayal as an Intense Experience

No matter how complicated the issue seems from a distance, when we have been betrayed or have betrayed, we know it. Betraying does not only cause strong indignation on the part of the observers but intense experiences for those involved. Due to the basicness of these feelings, as referred to initially by Bateson (1977), this aspect of the issue should be discussed. One facet of the intensity is indicated by the permanency. A betrayal event stays in people's minds, sometimes for a lifetime; and the experience often can be painful. "Et tu, Brute" is not only famous for

catching a historical incident or a saying, but for expressing a bitterness –
the final letdown. However, treachery as it is used here does not only
involve such final letdowns – it is used to include a wider area of behavior.
Betrayal in everyday life, even if only consisting of small-time happenings,
is still deeply and intensively felt.

To take but a few examples. A friend of mine had to undergo surgery
as a child. When she tells about this incident, it is not the surgery in itself
that is her point, it is the fact that her mother left her with the doctors,
"teamed up" with them instead of her. I think it is significant that she has
told me that story not once but several times and that it still seems to hurt
a bit every time. I believe many of us can recollect similar experiences of
betrayal where the event was not the main aspect; but rather, a basic
relationship of trust was shattered – even if put back together again
afterwards and the motives, especially if well-meaning as above, were
understood.

It can be painful not only to be the victim of a betrayal; that is, the
betrayed; but being the betrayer can also hurt. Associations of guilt or
shame can linger on long after the act took place.[23] Using the example
above, I imagine that most parents, if they had to do what my friend's
mother did, experience something akin to betrayal. Experiences of being
betrayed or being a betrayer are, of course, very subjective and dependent
on personalities. It also depends on how we perceive the victim: the more
defenseless and innocent, the more guilt we tend to experience.[24] As an
example, one woman I know is a stout defender of animals. Although
usually a mild, understanding woman she becomes quite vengeful when
she hears that defenseless and innocent animals are mistreated. She sees
herself as a "traitor" because she once tricked a cat she was taking care of
to come out from under the bed where it had hidden when the owners
came to collect it. It was not that she disapproved of the owners, but she
had betrayed the cat through trickery and she claimed she was the only
person the cat trusted. She used the word "traitor" and she cried when she
told about the incident, claiming she would never forget it.

The intensity of the experiences of betrayal are not only a matter of
personality or perception of the victim, but are also a matter of context.
In some contexts, such as so-called "suspicion awareness contexts" (Case
1987), betrayal may be seen as "a risk of the trade" rather than a deeply
felt experience occasioning remorse or pain. In a book about a man who
informed on his former Mafia associates, it is said:

> Of course, no matter how Henry tried to rationalize what he had done,
> his survival depended upon his capacity for betrayal. He willingly
> turned on the world he knew and the men with whom he had been

raised with the same nonchalance he had used in setting up a bookie joint or slipping a tail. For Henry Hill giving up the life was hard, but giving up his friends was easy. (Pileggi 1985, 274)

This man was raised with the friends he betrayed, but he lived with them in a culture where you were trained to be indifferent to violence and unpredictable punishment. Various forms of betrayal were not unusual and the main theme seemed to be about survival and individual success.

Seen in this light, betrayal in circumstances when it is not expected may be more painful than when it occurs in "suspicious awareness" contexts such as that of criminals or spies, even if practically it is not of great consequence. In more ordinary situations, the loss of a friend as a result of a betrayal or the realization in general that one cannot always expect even our parents or best friends to be infinitely loyal, may mean more: the We's of our lives are not forever.

One of the reasons for such intense feelings are the fact that if trust is broken when it is not expected to be, relations based on routine and taken for granted, which result in nonstrained interactions, are destroyed. Thus the consequence of betrayal in familiar contexts is, as Luhmann has pointed out, that the familiar itself is shattered:

. . . closer familiarity keeps the problem of trust from even becoming a matter for reflection. And when reflection does occur in such circumstances, its first victim is precisely familiarity in the sense of taking things utterly for granted. A gulf of unfamiliarity opens up even with respect to things and people nearest to one, which doubt removes into a surprising strangeness. (1979, 33)

Now, one may contrast seriousness of betrayal with the intensity of feelings of such betrayal. Doing this, one may suspect that most people would judge the treachery of a traitor to a country as having more serious consequences than that of friend betraying friend. In a social-psychological sense, however, the latter – or similar everyday life betrayals – is probably experienced and condemned more intensely. The Swedes who have been caught spying for other countries during the last years have certainly gained large media coverage. To my memory, however, none of them has been the object of many letters to the editor, coffee-room informal talks, etc. or if discussed, not in a heated way. They have passed on documents that do not mean too much to us (as ordinary citizens) and they appear more as mysterious, perhaps tragic, figures. Parenthetically, it is interesting to note that when such attitudes take the form of detached admiration, as in some films of Philby who actually sent many people to their deaths, some commentators (King 1989; Grenier 1985) feel the need to remind the public that condemnation (if not necessarily intense) would be more proper. The film critic Grenier wryly notes, for example, apropos some recently released films in his article "Treason Chic":

> Treason is in style. At least British treason. Or at least British treason when it is committed by Englishmen with posh accents wearing old Etonian ties. There is something poignant, and nostalgic, and bittersweet about it – to the point where all three of the leading British film imports into the U.S. in the last several months have wildly romanticized fictional creations suggested by the lives of Guy Burgess, Donald Maclean, and Kim Philby, Britain's three most famous, and infamous, traitors of the last half-century. (1985, 61)

Using the Dynamite in "Treason"

Betrayal may cause intense feelings and/or serious consequences. It is therefore naturally inviting to attempt to manipulate a situation by producing suspicions or "steering" in a climate angered or frightened by the issue of betraying. "Games of betrayal" can be seen both at a societal and an individual level.

Some societies make, create, or produce more betrayers than others because of the way their social control is arranged. All societies demand that citizens report on each other to a certain extent. How much and the range of behavior expected to be reported varies between countries. In some countries only strictly illegal behavior should be reported. In others, information concerning a much broader range of behavior is not considered private; on the contrary, it should be revealed to different authorities. After the turmoil following the student demonstrations in China in 1989, such aspects of everyday life informer systems have been given some publicity. It was explained, for example, how the old women whose jobs were to pass on all information of the happenings in a neighborhood could help catch those student leaders that had managed to escaped. (*Sydsvenska Dagbladet* /Swedish daily/ September 2, 1989, 14) The more totalitarian and the more interested their leaders are in suppressing criticism, the more such informer systems will be used. An informer system is not only a means of collecting information, but its most effective social function perhaps is the general fear it produces.[25]

From the perspective of those who point the finger at particular others, this action can serve two social functions: one by the finding of a scapegoat and the other by getting rid of undesirables. Blaming failures or embarrassing situations on the betrayer diverts the interest from other possible faults and focuses the attention on a specific individual or a certain stratum or group in a society. As to the latter, the German National Socialist slogan "Dolchsloss von hinten" (the stab in the back) that referred to the actions of the Social Democratic Party at the end of the World War I in 1918, may serve as an example.

There is also more direct uses in labeling someone a betrayer, as when one applies the label to score a point in a conflict, or to get rid of potential threats. Defining some acts as treacherous may minimize the risk of them being committed. Such uses may be so blatantly strategic that they do not win response among the public but are still effective ways of getting rid of undesirables. Naming a group or an individual collaborator(s) or scab(s) can be convincing arguments in a conflict. Examples of people with power using the label strategically are legion. To take some very different illustrations: Henry VIII used the label of traitor to get rid of competitors and de Gaulle was said to have done the same after the liberation.[26]

Turning to the perspective of individuals who betray – they may also play the game of betrayal quite consciously. In spy literature, for example, one speaks about the MICE-factor. Some of its ingredients can certainly be used quite instrumental as it refers to money, ideology, compromise, ego. (Pincher 1987, xiv) I would like however to point to Simmel's analysis again. He has written about "the fascination of betrayal" – our wish to capture the excitement of the moment when we divulge a secret. Revealing, telling, or leaving can be used as methods for extending a We or creating new social bonds. Such betrayals may also serve to maintain a social bond, as when we feel obliged to share a secret, even if we do not strictly have to or even if we should not. At times we endanger a We because we cannot refrain from using the secret to capture, hold, and be the star of the moment. To quote Aubert once again:

> . . . there were those to whom information seemed so attractive that they could not check their curiosity when opportunities presented themselves, nor could they refrain from disclosing their important "inside" status by information leaks and gossip. In general there was a gap between proclaimed principles and actual practice with respect to secrecy. Everybody knew that secrecy was vital; every new arrest would impress that upon the underground. But for young people, often isolated from normal social contacts, the need for intimacy and friendship encouraged gossip, and often a spontaneous revelation of real identity as the supreme token of unlimited mutual trust. (1965, 296)

Discussion

So far the centrality of betrayal has been discussed in connection with people's experiences with it. These experiences are characterized by their intensity and longevity; the memory of betrayal may stay in people's minds for a long time. In the following chapter issues such as how societies and groups are permeated with strategies and rules established to avoid treachery will be discussed. Evidence of the centrality will also be shown in how the issue is subject to recurrent discussions – who is really a betrayer and what is a betrayal? The strong norms surrounding the issue will be shown in that even those who benefit from the betrayal often reject the betrayer. These are all examples of the importance of the subject as a vital human concern.

I would like to end this chapter with emphasizing the *sociological* centrality. Circumstances in which the attribution of "betrayer" is applied makes it visible when a We – a society, a common religion or class, a group, a pair – is especially important. The analysis of betrayal also points out what a We is constituted of: the values, experiences, and common background that are deemed sacred. Formations of We's and the competitions between We's are made manifest through the theme of treachery. Furthermore, "the sociology of treachery" tells us about central features in the relation between these We's and that of the individual I, and the rivalries between these entities. In other words the study of treachery contains that which much of sociology is all about – solidarity, and its limits and boundaries.

Notes

1. A summarized description from Pincher (1987, 298).
2. The concept of trust is used here as a belief that the expectations we put in the We will be met. The expectations discussed here must be positive in some way. We hardly feel betrayed when not being hit by a man we know to be violent when drunk, for example. Moreover, trust here has a special association with expectations of agreed-on norms or understandings as to what is not to be revealed and what of our common information and knowledge is to be honored. Thus trust in this sense does not mean trusting someone to give good advice. It does not exclusively mean the breach of confidence. We therefore trust or expect not only that secrets are kept but also that when we form a group, even if temporarily, it will be honored at least by our physically staying within it.
3. Obviously there are analyses of such groups, but I have been unable to find the subject thematized as forms of betrayal. When searching for

material on "treachery," "traitors"," "betrayal," "betrayers," etc., the little I came up with dealt mostly with patriotic treachery or police informers.

4. How the organization should look was an issue of debate between those in exile and those in Norway. The former argued that the organization should be built on a central leadership, governed from abroad with local spies in Norway reporting directly to the leaders in exile. For security reasons those local spies would not have any internal contact. The other alternative, argued by the home front, was that the organization, leaders and all, should be placed in Norway since they had the experience and expertise. (Aubert 1965)

5. Collusion is sociologically interesting: even if we know it to take place, we would be hurt if the things our mutual friends talk about concerning us were stated publicly or if we happened to listen in by chance. (Here is one of the explanations why we feel awkward if two people we know suddenly stop talking when we arrive. We may suspect collusion yet it may only be the manner they collect themselves for integrating a new person in the team.) Collusion in everyday life, on a small-talk level, is in a way a betrayal and yet it is not, since we, by hiding it, assure it is not. It can be seen as a way of avoiding betrayal. Furthermore, collusion of this kind has its rules – it is thus not only the talked-about that would be embarrassed if the conversation got too open but also the others outside the group or a twosome. To share confidences, judgments on friends, etc., too openly would be met with distaste by others. "It's just not done. . ."

6. This was the case in Wieder's (1974) study of a halfway home for addicts. Among them the "code" stated that one was to minimize talking to the staff, even on trivial matters.

7. Usually these experiences of betraying versus being betrayed are probably fleeting, but in some contexts they may be articulated. One example of a student doing field observations on a religious sect is illustrative: "This problem of involvement was particularly bothersome to me. It was not necessarily the fact of how much I considered it necessary to become involved to get the data I wanted, nor how far the sect would let me go; but most of all it was a personal problem of how far I would allow myself to go. There was, of course, my own conscience and my own moral evaluations. As to the former I was, after all, a spy and it was difficult to decide just how much of a traitor I would allow myself to be. Then too, . . . there was the question of just how much I would humiliate myself or go against my own personal evaluations just for the sake of scientific inquiry." (Junker 1960, 123)

8. Whether organized crime is really the "Mafia" we imagine (*i.e.* tight-nit highly organized family businesses) is a matter of debate in criminology. (Cf. Ianni [1972], Cressey [1977], for different points of view.) For the sake of simplicity, however, I shall refer to "the Mafia", instead of "the so-called Mafia," or something similar.

9. As to the treaty: the Germans were tricked into signing by promises that were not kept.
10. As to political organizations: the Kurdic PKK has murdered those who have defected. As to religious sects: the Scientologists harass ex-members. Both these groups have been much discussed in the Swedish media lately due to this type of behavior. Parenthetically, an interesting research object would perhaps be to compare those sects defining leaving as betrayal with those not making such a definition. Another research topic could be a study of the processes involved in the development of such definitions.
11. In Lottman's book several examples are given of how the influence of time changes the definition of treachery: small incidents were heavily punished in the beginning of the purge, while some comparatively serious treacheries were hardly punished at all several years later.
12. Lottman quotes Farge (1946).
13. Perhaps those labeled gossips are not considered "traitors" since they do not necessarily intend to hurt, but may do so by unintended slips. They mix the good and the bad and talk for social reasons. For an analysis of the gossip, cf. Haugen (1983).
14. Lawson, in her book *Adultery,* has analyzed this as "double betrayals" (1988, 16).
15. The song is "Go on home, girl." Composer is A. Alexander, Painted Desert Music Corp. BMI. Ry Cooder has recorded it on "Bop til you drop." 1979, Warner Bros.
16. Blum 1987, legend to picture no 29.
17. He had given some secret official documents to the Russians but claimed this was only done as part of a private diplomacy intended to foster peaceful relations between the countries. See Skagen (1985) for the arguments of those defending him.
18. The concept burn-out has been used by many, but it was Christina Maslach who made it well known by popularizing and thematizing the subject. For a critical discussion of earlier analyses of the burning-out process including Maslach's, see Asplund (1987). He opposes the conventional use that I refer to and emphasizes instead the hollowness and lack of feelings and reactions towards clients as humans as the meaningful content of the concept.
19. Hellesnes himself divides treachery in (a) betrayal of authority and (b) betrayal of one's group (of solidarity).
20. A recent contribution to such discussions is King's (1989) differentiation of traitors as von Stauffenberg who attempted to assassinate Hitler and traitors such as the "Cambridge spies." In such comparisons one distinguishes between the legal and the moral. The reason for such distinctions are, I believe, that sometimes one do not grant the law makers real membership in a We. Another example of someone considering such distinctions is the author Rebecca West who wrestled with the concept of treachery after World War II. According to the author treason is usually wrong: a state gives its

citizens protection, in return it has a claim to their allegiancies. It may, however, be commendable: a form of necessary rebellion to promote social change and to defend private liberties. Yet another example can be taken from the journalist Pincher. He points toward the problem of those who change their We and he places some weight on whether this is done openly or not. He writes about a RAF flying officer, Anthony Wraight, who quite openly flew to Berlin, took the underground to the Eastern sector, and after making a pro-communist broadcast, was flown to Moscow. He then provided secret information about British aircrafts and weapons to the Soviet Union. (Pincher 1987, 13–14.) Considering that this man had changed his homeland and citizenship to another, Pincher asks: "Does he therefore have a right, or even perhaps the duty, to help his new country by imparting any secrets of special interest...?" (1987, 13)

21. Goffman uses this incident to illustrate "misplaced confidence." (1986, 121) Thus confidence or trust may be there and it may be breached; but if misplaced, it seems to lose the meaning of betrayal. Levinson (1983) has discussed different informers along these lines in connection to undercover agents versus "true informers."

22. Akin to this is the issue whether the "sleeping spy" – the one brought up in one country while maintaining loyalty all the time to another country – is a betrayer or not.

23. A drastic illustration is that according to many descriptions of (and by) those who survived the Nazi concentration camps such lifelong feelings of guilt, among people who often had no choice but to betray, are common. Cf. Levi (1988, 60–64).

24. Guilt may also be a matter of a changed definition of the victim. The process involved may include a beginning with feelings of guilt and an end with more uncomplicated dissociating/anger as a result of leaving the loyalty bond. For example, if we start to distance ourselves from a friend because we are disappointed or angry with him or her, we initially probably feel bad if we vent these feelings in talks with others. If the friend continues to confirm our disappointment or anger (perhaps because he or she feels our distrust), we may after some time vent such feelings without too much shame.

25. Many of the comments from citizens in the Eastern bloc, reported in the media, have concerned the relief in being free from fear after the break down of the communist machinery in 1989–1990 – thereby getting rid of the informer systems.

26. On Henry VIII, cf. Smith (1954) and on the internment of La Rocque, a political leader, as de Gaulle's way of rendering harmless a competitor, see Lottman (1986, 188–193).

2

Third Party Views
Trusted Ally or Despised Associate?

> *"Now why should I respect an informer? He's*
> *helping me do my job, in a sense, but yet I don't*
> *respect an informer. He violated the codes of his*
> *group . . ."* (member of staff from a halfway
> house for addicts, Wieder 1974, 152).

The above quote is illustrative of quite a usual attitude toward informers. This attitude is intriguing, as indicated in the quote, since it exists even when informers are instrumental: helping policemen do their jobs, generals win their wars, and so on. This chapter explores the third party's attitude, where the third party is "the one told to." Informing occurs in a constellation consisting of three parties – a triad. There is a betrayer, a betrayed, and the recipient of the betrayal. The theme to be discussed here is the third party's differing opinions concerning informers. Even if examples of the kind above – contemptuous – seem to be the most basic, some informers are hailed by their recipients. This happened for example during the McCarthy era.[1] Furthermore, examples of ambivalence – simultaneously expressed sympathy and contempt – can also be found toward informers. This was the case, for example, among some interviewed policemen.

The differing perspectives on the informer is viewed as being a result of the moral context and the attributed motives for informing. The basic moral or "ideational notion"[2] toward informers is, I believe, negative. This is the prescribed attitude. Real life, however, makes room for negotiation and exceptions – a stretching of morals.

In the following, I shall discuss the third party, as mentioned above. The empirical material I have gathered myself consists of interviews with

27

police and prison staff. Consequently a rather large part of the discussion will concentrate on their views. Other material is collected from secondary sources with varying contents.

The General Contempt

The contempt toward informers by the third party can be found in numerous places. In classic legends and in historical accounts, for instance, one can easily find examples that seem to indicate that the issue of betrayers is a general or basic human concern, transcending cultures and time.[3] Famous historical figures as Cicero and Tacitus are reported to have stated respectively, "No wise man ever thought that a traitor could be trusted" and "Betrayers are hated even by those whom they benefit." (Stevenson's Book of Quotations 1934, 2034, 2033).

Mythology can be used to point out some of the themes inherent in this contempt. One case illustration from the world of Nordic mythology is the story of Balder and Loki. Loki discovered through trickery that Balder – the favorite of the gods – was invulnerable to everything living except mistletoe. Jealous of Balder and wishing his death, Loki gave an arrow made of mistletoe to a blind god and tricked him into throwing it at Balder, thus mortally wounding him. The same Loki was befriended by Thor, the god of thunder, and rescued from many perils. Yet Loki did not hesitate to betray Thor to the giant Geirröd in order to save his own skin.[4] From this story one learns that the propensity for betrayal is a persistent flaw in personal character. It is not a one-time activity, it is repetitive.

In Greek mythology, stories of betrayal are common. The moral lessons often point out the futility for the betrayer: sins like these do not pay. In one legend, Theseus, prince of Athens, was sent to Crete to defeat the dreaded Minotaur. Ariadne, daughter of King Minos of Crete, fell in love with Theseus and helped him (thereby betraying her father's trust). After killing the Minotaur Theseus fled Crete with Ariadne, only to abandon her on the island of Naxos when he decided he preferred her sister, Phaedra.[5] The Battle of Thermopylae is a further example. It would not have been won by the invading army of Persians in 480 BC if the Greeks had not been betrayed by a fellow Greek, Ephialtes, who, hoping for wealth and fame, told the Persian king Xerxes about the mountain path that let the Persians troops in behind the defending Greeks. The Greeks were killed to the last man – including Ephialtes.[6]

Turning to modern times the last World War naturally provides us with many examples. The typical one perhaps concerns Hitler, who was said to have looked on Quisling with contempt. (Rieber-Mohn, 1969, 32; Hayes 1971, 292; Littlejohn, 1972, 51) One of Quisling's associates wrote in a letter in 1945 that not only Hitler himself but the German authorities held the same attitudes: "I have a feeling that the German authorities are deliberately making fools of you . . . and of the *Nasjonal Samling*. . . . Under a pretence of friendship and co-operation, they manage to make our administration share their guilt as plunderers and oppressors." (Quoted in Andenaes, 1966, 79)

Another illustration is that of the Germans' view of Roger Casement, an Irishman who worked for England as a diplomat in the Foreign Service, but who later devoted himself to the cause of Irish independence and was ultimately executed for planning collaboration between Germany and Ireland against England. Rieber-Mohn expresses the role of this type of betrayer well:

Casement's role among the Germans is a pathetic example of the helplessness of the traitor. His lack of rights turns to dependency. His new masters exploit him ruthlessly – often with barely concealed contempt. No one is faithful to the faithless – he is neither fish nor fowl. He is declared an outlaw, abandoned, seldom a factor to be reckoned with. No one takes responsibility for him – he is only *used*. (Rieber-Mohn 1969, 32; my translation)

It is important to note that attitudes like these are not just thoughts or values of little importance and with no real effects. They can lead to real, concrete, and vital consequences not only for the informer but for others as well. The possibility of such attitudes to influence the third party's treatment of informers can be seen in various circumstances. Here, one aspect of this will be illustrated: the unwillingness to act on the word of an informer. During World War II the British military attaché in Switzerland is reported to have dismissed a German clerk, Mr. Kolbe, who had brought important diplomatic cables from the German Foreign Office: "Angered by what he saw as a miserable German trying to ingratiate himself because his country was losing the war, Cartwright dismissed him without a proper hearing." (Pincher 1987, 27) It is interesting to note that Kolbe was later called "the intelligence officer's dream." The information was received by an American intelligence chief in Bern, Allen Dulles, who was "impressed because Kolbe never asked for money." (Ibid.)

In other words, in a situation like this it might not be sufficient to bring information while risking one's life. It might also be important to show the right moral fiber (for example, not to ask for a reward) in order, as in this case, to be believed at all and certainly to gain respect from the third party.

In the empirical studies I have carried out concerning criminals, the natural "third party" - the police and prison staff - also reaps the benefit of the informer's information but holds some of the same general negative views. In a prison study we asked the staff about how they dealt with informers. (Åkerström 1985b, 24) This guard's rather tough attitude was not uncommon:

> "Are there stoolies [here]?"
> "Yeah, of course, but we gotta protect them."
> "You have to take care of them?"
> "Yeah, but we don't exactly respect them - you can't. There's nothing honest or straight in 'em."
> "Why do they snitch?"
> "They do it to get in good - they think they'll get some benefits."

In this interview it is clear that the interviewee not only looked down on the informer but also morally questioned his motives.[7] In another interview a variation on the theme of nontrustworthiness in general, that is, the doubting of the value of their information, is evidenced. This is probably especially common when information is volunteered and not asked for. Here one comes closer to the role of the busybody - never a social star. A prison guard stated: "We've had inmates who've talked a whole lot, but we don't like it either - you never know what's the truth and what's a lie when they come and tell you stuff." (Åkerström 1985, 24)

Negative stereotyping of informers by the police has been documented in studies and books on policemen. (See for example Van Maanen 1988; Lidz and Walker 1980; Harney and Cross 1960). In my interviews with policemen, the moral issue was not as one-dimensional. They were often more ambivalent. However, the reverse moral code was seen here since those who refused to talk won respect:

> "There're a lot who never budge, who would never even *dream* óf. . . . Take for example Stor-Olle [a local well-known fence and drug pusher] - he'd never dream of squealing on someone. He was really straight where that was concerned. He *never* talked about others."

Or:

> "Just try to get a guy to talk who's been in jail a couple of times and knows the laws of the underworld. It's tough . . . and in a way you gotta hand it to 'em. 'Cause they stick by their own. They're not rats. Put

yourself in their place and imagine if as a criminal you had some partner you couldn't trust. Think how pissed off you'd be at him."

Some policemen have even felt it necessary to remind some of their colleagues that if one wished to use informers in the future, one had to protect them and keep one's promises. (Harney and Cross 1960) They condemned policemen who thought it unnecessary to be honest with informers since the latter were disloyal and dishonest themselves.

It is interesting to observe that the contempt of the third party is noted and perhaps used by members of the betrayable We. While interviewing prison inmates, it was apparent that the negative attitude of the police and the prison staff was a "known fact."[8] One illustration from an interview I did with a woman inmate:

"Do they [the police] respect or despise informers?"
"Cops don't like stoolies. They're not particularly popular."
"What about the staff [at prison]?"
"There's nothing worse than canaries."

While discussing the general contempt toward informers, I would like to add one more aspect. It has been said above that contempt may have real consequences. One facet is, of course, the fate of informers. On the one hand, the police and prison staff claim to protect their sources. They emphasize the value of mutual trust and in not breaking promises. They also underline the importance of protecting informers as best as they can. When talking about this, the interview climate changes. Employed strategies are talked about with a somewhat secretive and confidential – even mystifying – air. Although this is difficult to convey because quotes cannot illustrate atmosphere, it is clear by the way voices are lowered, etc. The prison staff or police who deal with informers seem eager to present themselves as smart and sophisticated in this respect: they recount elaborate strategies, employed tactical reasoning, and so on. On the other hand, even if they sometimes succeed in acting as they say they do when dealing with informers concretely, some "sloppy" or indifferent behavior was noted. Some of the protective cover-ups for the safety of the informer were routinely used and thus easily recognized by other criminals. Sometimes the police or prison staff did not bother to check whether these strategies helped to shield the informer. We have encountered many such instances. One example will perhaps suffice. While doing research in prison, the "drug search patrol" (a quasi-police group comprised of prison guards) let me speak to one of their informers. The men in the patrol had earlier told me how they arranged discrete and secret meetings with their informants. Now they made a clumsy and simple mistake in the way they let the two of us meet by simply ordering him down to their office. Since he was not known to be an addict, associating with the patrol was, to put it mildly, suspicious in the eyes of his fellow inmates. He was scared to death and asked me if I could not come back as "a visitor" to meet with him in the guest room because the other inmates at the ward had naturally become suspicious about him being called down by the feared patrol.

A few aspects of the tendency towards contempt that have been illustrated above will now be discussed. In my interviews I noted, for example, that the contempt did not need to be "backed up." Explanations or stories of how informers had been unreliable in the police and prison staff's past experiences were not given. This does not mean that if asked, answers would not have been given; but the lack of such legitimations seems to indicate that they were not deemed necessary. Being an informer is equated with being bad.

Badness in this case seems to indicate something "sneaky." This underhandedness expresses itself in various forms. In the popular view informers are, I believe, thought of as being sly and as working in the dark – one is "stabbed in the back" by them. Another, quite interesting connotation is evidenced in some of the examples above. This is the "once a betrayer, always a betrayer"-belief.[9] Not even the third party whom they have helped can be sure of their loyalty. Loyalty thus seems to be seen as a trait, that once cracked is beyond repair. Informers are generally considered untrustworthy; one could not depend on such a person to pay debts, or they were ascribed other seemingly unconnected characteristics. (Åkerström 1985b) In other words being an informer seemed to be what Hughes named a master status. (1984, 147) Being unreliable in other ways than the one-time betrayal can be deemed the auxiliary characteristics of the role of the "rat."

The negative attitudes toward informers can be viewed as an upholding of the value of loyalty – a value whose relation to other moral commandments ("oughts") is interesting. In many instances being loyal is preferable to being honest. This is obviously so concerning "white lies," smaller sins, etc., but also concerning more serious matters. The third party may share this ranking of values, as has been exemplified above when policemen even if only at an "attitude-level" prefer those telling lies rather than those telling truths about their criminal colleagues. Another value that is shown to be secondary in priority is to show gratitude for received help. In the cases discussed so far, the third party did not follow this social rule.

The initial issue regards contempt versus the gain of the information in relation to informers. If one viewed people as instrumental or rational in a simplistic way, they would in an unquestioning, undemanding manner appreciate those who gave them help, that is information. However, perceiving the value of loyalty as a very fundamental human concern, it would be hard to liberate oneself from the massive moral rejection of those who break this value. Against this background it is reasonable that the contempt is shared also by those who do not belong to the betrayed.

Given this contempt, the chance of acting it out by showing it or by failing to protect the informer must be greatly enhanced by the low risk this involves. This is so because most informers are placed in a position where they no longer have a supporting group from which to rally their demands or to which to vent their grievances.

All such rules or norms have their exception. This will be discussed below.

The Stretching of Morals

Portraying the third party as only contemptuous would be a simplification. "Ideational" morality here, as is often the case, is modified by reality. Reality allows a "stretching" of values, and the individual hence tends to "negotiate" with himself or with others. Let's take a look at the answer I received in an interview with a police officer:

"The word tjallare [slang for informer] – what does it represent?"[10]

"It's sort of ambiguous. If I look at it from the point of view of my work, it's someone I benefit a lot from. But in my private life, it's not so great. . . . But as a policeman, I'm so into my work and it's so important that if the truth be known I think it more than compensates for the fact that we use tjallare as an important instrument in our work. . . . Even if as a man I may think it's sort of too bad that he has to come forward as a tjallare. You get a little ambivalent."

"You try to turn someone into a tjallare but then feel a little sorry that he's become one?"

"Yeah, in some of the cases."

The resulting attitudes toward informers may, as in the quote above, be a mixture of both an ideational norm, the real, concrete persons one gets to know, and the situation where one meets them. The ingredients can consist of informers as useful tools but no good as a general category; some generate sympathy and therefore one regrets having made them odious. These attitudes may exist side by side, which makes for, as the policeman said, an ambivalence.

As is true for other stereotypes, *face to face contacts* have the power of changing or revising them. (Berger and Luckmann 1972) In this case, the stereotypes are perhaps so negative initially that any revision of them is likely to be positive. If placed in a situation of face-to-face interaction with informers, they have the opportunity to present themselves as ordinary people whose motives are understandable and possible to sympathize with. While interviewing ordinary prison staff[11] (that is, those working with inmates directly), I believe there was a marked difference among those who handled protected inmates, among them snitches, and those working with ordinary inmates. The former's attitude was more matter-of-fact. They talked about the informers as people who had "talked too much in court or to the police." And that was it. Sometimes they added a sympathetic explanation, like "the police put a lot of pressure on them." We never encountered statements about snitches as sneaky types, greedy, or mostly interested in their own welfare, as happened among other guards.

Moreover, broadly speaking, there seemed to be a difference between policemen and prison staff in general. The blatant, contemptuous remarks we came across were more often expressed by prison staff than by policemen. This difference may be attributed to the different work situations of the police and the prison staff. The police need informers to a larger extent and sometimes "live off" them.[12]

Moreover, even if prison staff interact a lot with informers as measured in time, they do not associate as intensely or as closely with them as individuals as do the police. This distance may facilitate the adoption of a more simplistic tough attitude – an attitude furthermore sanctioned by general societal values.

A developing closeness can even arise between the informer and a policeman, when they have known each other for some time. While interviewing informers at prison some explained that "their" policeman had known them since they were kids and had helped them a lot even after being incarcerated. Perhaps it is more difficult for prison staff to form such special relationships since their everyday meetings with inmates take place from the point of view of a collective facing another collective.

Furthermore, the police appreciated those who agreed to testify in court. Such *openness* was a mitigating factor. It appears that nonpublic informers are bound to appear more suspicious.[13] Secrecy in itself seems to imply sneakiness. Obviously, the information given in such circumstances is more uncheckable. Openness is also associated with "taking a stand" and showing courage. Moreover, in a situation of openness, the pressure on the receiver of information to stand up for and defend the informer is apt to increase.

Another quite interesting social-psychological mitigating factor may be applicable in some contexts of informationseeking. These are the cases where a strong line is not deemed fruitful, where it at least needs to be mixed with more positive measures. These do not need to be explicit. According to my own interviews as well as some American police studies (Skolnick 1967; Lidz and Walker 1980) and in a book on interrogation and confessions (Inbau and Reid 1962), one emphasizes *showing respect* as a strategy. In those studies the police are said to use strategies to mitigate or lower the stigmatizing identity of being a "snitcher." One does this by showing respect and taking an interest in those one recruits through one's own general conduct, by inquiring about their family, their health, and through one's choice of words and manner of speaking. A fair speculation is that these techniques may have a latent function in lessening possible previous negative attitudes.[14]

Informers as Work

Initially I was intrigued by some policemen being contemptuous while simultaneously claiming it was necessary to create a trusting relationship with informers. However, it may be that these stands were not very deeply felt or held. In many of the situations where policemen deal with informers, they may not need to integrate these "levels." The negative stereotypes may on the one hand be quite superficial, not very deeply felt; and on the other, the positive feelings that should result from the humanizing aspects of trust and understanding may be easily adopted because relations are mostly short and businesslike.

Perhaps a common way of viewing informers among groups that have to recruit them, such as the police, is mostly that of a "scalp" view? That is counting success in terms of numbers and quality of those acquired. If this is the case, neither contempt nor sympathy is very relevant. Some police studies seem to indicate this. The scalp view arises because informers in much of policework are essential, and thus become not only an aid to but also a sign of success in one's work. Contempt may exist but not be a vital element as is illustrated in a method discussion in an article on police research. The researcher has himself been a policeman and he describes how he is received by his former classmates from the police academy when he was about to study them several years later. He discusses the problem of "overrapport" – and describes how his former friends now want to demonstrate their acquired competence, showing off their "scalps" for his benefit.

I watched some of my former colleagues as they sought out, pushed around, and goaded several of their informants apparently only to demonstrate to me the fact that they now had their own intelligence networks – though to a man they thought their informants to be "scum." (Van Maanen 1988, 283)

Informers may also be purely instrumental, a mean of achieving a goal – not even underlying contempt or sympathy may be present. In the book *Heroin, Deviance and Morality* the role of the police is analyzed as well as their views to addicts. In their ideology the most important distinction is that between addicts and others. Thus we can find that informers play no big part as a role in their drama:

Addicts saw informing as a shameful activity, while the detectives saw it as dangerous. . . . Once when we were observing the vice squad trying to convince a young addict to inform on the man for whom he was dealing, the addict objected that "if I do, you guys won't respect me." The detective found his comment very funny. Their world view allowed little grounds for respect for any addict, informer or not, but the addict saw informing as shameful and expected the detectives to see it that way as well. (Lidz and Walker 1980, 128–129)

Also according to the authors quoted above, informers are essential in the sense that they count as the most important aspect of the prestige hierarchy among vice-squad detectives. The quantity and quality of the detectives' informants are deemed important and ". . . enormous amounts of time and effort were put into developing and maintaining informants." (Lidz and Walker 1980, 137)

Even if there is such a declared view of professionalism, one may regret adopting this perspective towards others. There may still be room for ambivalence. In a book by a former Scotland Yard police officer this is evident. He regrets the transformation in himself which has made him view people more as instruments of getting information than "people" who deserve at least some sympathy. In his autobiography this feeling is conveyed. He tells about how in the beginning of his career he thought it was unpleasant when a thief was sentenced in court. His success in having caught the thief ". . . turns to ashes in my mouth." There is perhaps a crying wife in the court and he knows about

. . . the struggle there'll be to buy groceries and pay the rent. So I go backstage, as it were, and fork out a little cash. . . . In my later career my natural sympathy was tempered by a ruthless mind. Behind the generosity there was also an eye to the main chance. A good deed today might pay dividends in the future. Today's thief might be tomorrow's informer, and a few more villains might bite the dust. But it wasn't like that in the beginning. . . . (Gosling 1959, 34)

Redefinitions

So far we have dealt with general contempt toward informers as a basic attitude, how this view can be mitigated, and finally how neither contempt nor sympathy may be relevant if informers are strictly seen as part of one's work. Now we will take a look at the fact that informers can in fact not only be "understood in spite of. . ." but that they can be viewed as respectable people or even heroes as well.

Some informers are given the role of heroes rather unquestioningly, as has been discussed elsewhere in this book. These are whistleblowers or revealers of what Goffman (1959, 141) labeled dirty secrets. Other such informers who are more or less automatically transformed into heroes are those whom one believes act for sincere moral motives, not betraying their true We, and even better, while taking personal risks. Typical examples from the Allies' point of view would be the Germans during World War II who informed about Nazi activities. Their help to the Allies was justified because Germany during Nazi rule was not seen as the true Germany.[15]

In other cases if one wants to change the image of the informer it has to be, so to say, converted or transformed. During the McCarthy era it was attempted to actively turn informers into becoming heroes. Some of those witnesses were themselves instrumental in redefining the label. Wittaker Chambers for example argued that informing was an act of penance; and according to Navasky: ". . . he helped to bring about the metamorphosis of the informer's image from rat to lion, from stoolie to patriot." (1982, xxii) A commentator who worried about this process taking place stated:

Today scores of political informers, most of them ex-Communists, have become circuit-riding witnesses, appearing again and again. . . . The demand for the services of political informers is fed by the frequently sensational stories they tell on the witness stand. . . . The political informer has become the star witness – the main attraction – in the circus-like hearings. (Donner 1954, 298)

The role reversal by itself, the glorification of "tale-bearers" could even be interpreted as jeopardizing one of the basic moral fibers of society. Another commentator stated: "I am disturbed by the growing inclination to turn spies into heroes. One of the earliest lessons learned by children is that tale-bearing is a dirty business." (Chafee 1952, 618)

Another illustration of attempts to redefine the image of the informer is recounted by Radzinowicz in *A History of English Criminal Law*. There he tells about a movement for correcting the manners of the lower classes during the late seventeenth and mid-eighteenth centuries. (vol. II. 1956, 2–18) Idleness, drunkenness, and so on were seen as immediate causes of crimes. Several "Societies for Reformation" were established. Sermons were held in their favor, and they were supported by the highest quarters. Queen Anne supported them, as did the Archbishop. The societies prosecuted people, on information gained from informers, for such transgressions as swearing, cursing, and breaking the Sabbath.

> To inform about breaches of the laws against vice they held to be a duty of all sober Christians and good neighbours. The objection that to be an informer was unworthy of a gentleman or good neighbour was brushed aside. To withhold information when "the Truth contributes to the bearing down of Sin, is to serve the Devil. . . and deny that Service that is due to God." (Radzinowicz 1956, 15)

The fact that some selected groups took this stance toward informers was not popular among the public at large. The position taken by the Societies for Reformation was not only criticized by intellectuals such as Defoe but was physically endangering. The societies were so hated that some of their members were murdered.

Clashes between the third party and other interested parties, for example, the public, may go in the opposite direction as well. In these cases the public may find the third party too callous. Such cases are those where one fails to protect someone who has informed but is seen as "good" and vulnerable. An illustration to such a reaction was given in a newspaper story about a girl previously addicted to drugs. She had decided to "come clean" in order to quit her addiction. She went voluntarily to the police, without being a suspect, confessed to earlier crimes, and told about former associates. She was sentenced to three years' imprisonment. The newspaper reported that she was now afraid of her fellow inmates' reprisals and that the Correctional Board had declared that they could not protect her. After the story was run, the paper followed up the article by reporting that they had received numerous letters from aggrieved readers and quoted a few. For example: "You write that you want to pay your debt to society. You have no debt. It is you who are the victim for all the ones who are guilty." And: "What an admirable person you are. Don't give up." (*Expressen*/Swedish daily/March 16, 1989, p. 8)

Language as a Definition-Changing Tool

Informer is not a neutral word – on the contrary, it is loaded with negative associations. In the case where the third party wishes to redefine its informant from a shadowy image to that of a good, dutiful citizen, the use of language seems to be very significant. Both in literature on betrayal and in my own interviews with policemen, examples are plentiful. The statements made by an English bishop from the eighteenth century and an American law enforcement officer from the twentieth, J. Edgar Hoover, former head of the FBI, are strikingly similar. Both felt a need to deal with the very word informer. The bishop defended those who served as informers for the earlier mentioned Societies of Reformation. In a sermon he emphasized that:

The word "informer" was only of a "middle nature," neither bad nor good, and there was nothing to be ashamed of, especially as "next to the fault of concealing Offenders, is not to discover them." (Radzinowicz 1956, 16; from the Lord Bishop of St. Asaph, January 5, 1730)

J. Edgar Hoover commented on those who criticized the people who served as witnesses to the Committee on Un-American Activities:

They stigmatize patriotic Americans with the obnoxious term "informer," when such citizens fulfill their obligations of citizenship by reporting known facts of the evil conspiracy to properly constituted authorities. (Donner 1973, 339–40)

In other contexts where the issue is not to glamourize informers, *le mot juste* is still important. When I was conducting interviews at prison I had gotten accustomed to categorizing every inmate who had given information about someone else to the police or to the prison staff as "tjallare" (negative slang for informer). This created some confusion when I first began talking to policemen. One high-ranking officer claimed that in his district (a large rural area) people did not "tjalla" – this he saw as an urban phenomenon. I thought he was being uncooperative, trying to prevent me from annoying his policemen with interviews. It was not until later interviews with city policemen that it became clear that many Swedish policemen tend to differentiate between the tellers as "tjallare" and others.[16] The others were not given any special label – they just "told" or "cooperated." For example, they consisted of those who tell about their associates during an interrogation. While such telling was clearly "tjallning" in prison society, it was not always considered as such by the police. Many policemen's definition of the 'tjallare' was that of someone who occupied this role on a more or less steady basis, being paid by monetary or legal means.

One illustration of how a policeman views informers appeared in a talk about possible rewards (such as being temporarily released from arrest prior to sentencing) for those passing on information about their associates. He took the opportunity to correct my use of language:

"And then they may talk [if given such releases], – yeah, they say that they made the break-in with the other one. And then it's often a sensitive point – they want to know who confessed first. In those cases they want a copy of the proceedings, and they read it very carefully. What the other said, and when. . . . You can't say in this kind of context that they tjallar on each other – it's more that they simply till it like it was to try to save their skins."

"Tjalla perhaps sounds nasty?"

"Yes, I think it's a heavy-duty word. You associate it immediately with people who profit economically by nailing their chums. Even though they're criminals themselves."

Discussion

The third party – the told to – often has a contemptuous attitude towards the informer, even when the betrayal may benefit him. Morals, however, can be altered or nuanced depending on context, the perceived character of the informer, and that of the group he betrays. The informer's closeness to his former We may be one important condition, since different degrees of loyalty are expected depending on the relationship to the core of the group. If the betrayed individual or group is viewed somewhat sympathetically – as some crooks can be viewed by the police – the betrayal itself tends to be met with contempt, much more so than if the group is uncategorically the enemy as in a war situation. However both these elements – the nature of the betrayer and of the betrayed – are important, dependent on each other, and somewhat interchangeable. Even if a policeman generally considers informers negative, he may be sympathetic if the informing is done for good moral reasons or if better still the information is given openly and not secretly. Similarly, during a war informers may not be considered heroes if they do not help the war effort while taking personal risks or for idealistic reasons.

Therefore, while informers are generally viewed with contempt not only by those they have betrayed but also by those who receive the information, mitigating factors are at work. The vocabulary alone is evidence of this. The police hestitate to use the word "tjallare" about those who reveal something about their associates during an interrogation. Those in the Resistance during World War II, who gave information to the West were not "snitches, traitors or informers" in the view of the third party. In short, the moral context can alter the moral fixture: informers are to be condemned since loyalty is a trans-time and trans-cultural value in its own right.

Notes

1. Cf. Chafee 1952; Donner 1954; and Navasky 1982.
2. Znaniecki (1952) differentiated between ideational attitudes: those expressed by a speaker or writer, and realistic attitudes; those expressed through action. Even though this is not equivalent to my use since the attitudes that were a result of negotiations were also spoken, the distinction is quite similar.
3. Judas is obviously the incarnation of the betrayer. However, he is not discussed since it is only the third party's view that is analyzed here. In the story of Judas the priests' attitude toward him is not the central theme.
4. *New Larousse Encyclopedia of Mythology*. 1959, 266, 268.
5. Ibid., p. 176.
6. Herodotus, VII, 201–228.
7. Whereas prison staff and others may question the motives of an informer because he expect favors, sometimes informers are more suspect because they do not ask for compensation in return for information. In a report from the National Police Board it was stated: "Sometimes an informer helps the police without asking for any compensation – more than the pleasure of being on their good side. Such a motivation should cause the police to be cautious – it could be an attempt to infiltrate." (SPANARKgruppen 1980, 46)
8. One possible consequence of this belief among criminals is that they may think that they have a license to harass informers. Another is that this belief may inhibit potential informers.
9. Not only informers seem to be portrayed as notoriously undependable; other betrayers share the same fate. In an "Advice to the Lovelorn" column, the columnist responded in a similar way to a woman having an affair with a married man who is now flirting with other women: "Well, what can I say that you don't already know, deep down? Sneaking around for ten years – what kind of love is that? And at a working place where even his wife is employed? If he cheats on her, why shouldn't he cheat on you?" (*Året Runt* /Swedish Magazine/ 11, March 13, 1989, 120)

10. This word has been translated in other places in the text with snitch, stool pigeon, rat or informer. It is a rather common slangword but is mostly used in connection with policemen and criminals. It is, at times, used in other contexts but it is not used, for example, among children. The reason I use the Swedish word here is because of a later discussion marking a difference in the use of the word between policemen and criminals. There is no Swedish word equivalent to "informer." The positive term would be a witness or the neutral an "information-giver." The latter, however, could be anyone outside the We. The police, however, did use an expression that referred to the behavior of informing, which was the same as the criminals used. This was that someone had "lagt någon" (something like being responsible for someone being convicted).

11. I exclude the administrators from this discussion because their views were often too polite and too abstract to be of interest in this context.

12. American prison studies often emphasize the need for informers in prisons to help control the inmate society. This is true here as well but to a lesser degree. The climate is much less violent. This is probably due to factors such as smaller prisons, often containing only fifty to onehundred prisoners, few ethnic tensions, more personnel, and much shorter sentences.

13. This can be compared to Navasky's (1982) account of the informers during the McCarthy period.

14. Compare Asplund (1987) in his discussion of feelings as results of behavior rather than the reverse.

15. I take it for granted that they were mostly seen as heroes by those who received their information, even if there were exceptions like that of Mr. Kolbe. That there still may be a tension between "traitor" and "resister" is evidenced, at least in fiction by the spy novelist Ted Allbeury. In connection to a discussion between some Germans about informing the British, he writes: ". . . the approach to the British; that was where they always hesitated. His brother Hans, von Stauffenberg, Beck and von Witzleben. They all said that it was crossing the line from being resisters to being traitors." (Allbeury 1981, 92–93)

16. See also Rubenstein (1978) for American patrolmen's distinctions of those giving information in the context of a neighborhood. Rubenstein furthermore gives interesting illustrations of how the position in the police organization determines the availability and restrictions in gaining information.

3

Heroes or Traitors?
A Social Role Allowing Two
Dramatic and Opposing Typings

Traitors and Heroes (Garbus 1987), *Patriot or Traitor – the case of general Mihailovitch* (Martin 1978), *Pétain – Hero or Traitor?* (Lottman 1985), *Patriotic Traitors – A History of Collaboration in German-Occupied Europe, 1940–1945* (Littlejohn 1972), *OB – Traitors or Patriots* (Visser 1976), *Silas Deane – Patriot or Traitor?* (James 1975), *Quislings or Realists – Documentary Study of Colored Politics in South Africa* (Hugo 1978)

The book titles above have one thing in common; namely, the theme of judging the same individual as good and bad. They clearly illustrate the duality of some betrayal roles in social typing: traitor/hero and collaborator/realist. The social type that most clearly illustrates the possibility of making heroes out of betrayers is the revealer of dark secrets, where the lifting of the veil is apt to be considered by some people to be a good thing. The revealer, commonly called "the whistleblower," is seen as a fruitful contrast to that betrayer-role that has been much discussed elsewhere in this book – the informer. Persons labeled one or the other both betray by telling, but they are cast in roles with very different moral connotations.

The Whistleblower as Hero and Traitor

Three cases of whistleblowers will be presented. All were labeled as traitors – informally or formally. It is largely the other side of the coin that will be discussed here; that is, the positive side for exposing that

43

which ought to be exposed. This good image differs between the three cases and ranges from hero to lonely crusader to martyr. As I see it, these different typings depend on two aspects. First, whether they are surrounded by a group supporting them – hailing and "catching" them – during their information-giving or not. The second aspect is whether the exposures were formally or officially punished or not.[1] (All the discussed revealers were informally punished through ostracism, anonymous threatening letters, etc.)

The martyrs are formally punished but may be supported and helped by groups or individuals *after* they have been punished for revealing damaging information. On the other hand heroes do not need help in this sense – he or she is not to be pitied. They will become or are already seen as representatives for a cause when they reveal their information. The lonely crusader is obviously not much supported and hence cannot make the status of a hero, but neither is he or she cast in the role of the martyr since no formal punishment follow their revealings. The differing fates of whistleblowers can be summarized through a typology:

	Supporting Group Behind	
Formal punishment	Yes	No
Yes	1. Hero	3. Martyr
No	2. Hero	4. Lonely Crusader

The cases that will illustrate the analysis are: Ingvar Bratt (type 2, hero), Stanley Adams (type 3, martyr) and Serpico (type 4, lonely crusader). Type 1 has not been included since I would imagine that it is not very much different from type 2. It should be added that heroes who are formally punished already have supporters at the time of their revealings and punishments.[2]

The information about the three revealers was gleaned mainly through their autobiographies. Bratt and Adams have themselves written about their affairs, while Serpico's story is written by Maas (1973).[3] The affairs and reactions toward the revealers are taken from the versions in the books. If I were seeking the absolute truth about these incidents, I would of course be making a methodological error. Since the purpose here is to present cases where the status of revealers differs, stylized versions of reality are judged to be sufficient.

The Case of Ingvar Bratt

"Is the leak a hero or a traitor?" This was a local editor's comment on the man who leaked the information about illegal sales of weapons by the Swedish weapon manufacturer Bofors. This affair was to become a Swedish variant of the American selling of arms to Iran in exchange for hostages. The company has close ties to the government; it is closely supervised and important for employment as well as export earnings. During the discussions of the affair there were speculations involving former Prime Minister Olof Palme, made piquant since he was known as a spokesman for peace. Furthermore, arms had been sold to Iran (forbidden by Swedish law since Iran was at war) where Palme was a mediator. This, coupled with a suicide[4] by a highly placed official in a governmental agency responsible for inspecting the export of weapons, guaranteed dramatic substance. The matter was highly sensitive.

What the local editor referred to was not the image of Bratt in Sweden in its entirety but as a hero to peace organizations and others, and equally as a traitor to the people in Karlskoga, the town where Bofors is situated, a town that is more or less dependent on the company for its survival. For this reason, emotions ran high when the "leak" stepped forward and unveiled his identity (in the beginning he secretly passed on information to a peace organization). The day after he openly presented his knowledge, the headlines in the local paper read as follows: "Ingvar dared to accuse Bofors – Karlskoga is worried about its jobs." (p. 107)[5] The journalist speculated on whether Bratt would dare to return to Bofors again. People in the streets of Karlskoga were also polled for their opinions. Most were negative and described him as "a fanatic" or someone who "is doing the wrong thing," a person who should have gone to the police if he had something to complain about.

When revealers go against the group, they may break the We or at least change it. Such behavior can be viewed as courageous or cowardly. These moral judgments are evidently important in the discussions and interpretations of Bratt's behavior. In the newspaper article above it is already evident. A person interviewed by the journalist states, "I think it was a courageous act if it was done for moral reasons." (p. 107) This latest comment, then, is the equivalent of the headlines above "Ingvar *dared* to accuse . . ." Some, however, see his behavior as cowardly: "Swedish companies need skilled and proper employees who are so loyal that they act within the framework of the company, unlike I.B., stabbing it in the back. I.B. wasn't brave enough. . . ." (letter to the local paper, p. 113) The theme of courage is also evident in the title of Bratt's book *Mot Rädslan (Against Fear)*.

In the school where he started to work as a teacher after quitting Bofors, his pupils are divided. Those who are critical concentrate, according to the book, on the employment situation. From a class discussion:

> "I don't agree with you," says one of the older pupils. "You should be loyal to your company. And what's going to happen to my job, which I'm supposed to start in two weeks at Bofors? Imagine if they take it away?" He was very upset. "What you did might leave 200 families without work," says another pupil. (p. 109)

Probably because of the attention the affair got in the media, the government passed further restrictions for the export of weapons, which led to Bofors' threatening to sack a substantial part of their work force. After this Bratt received threatening letters, some people spat when they saw him, and he needed a guard when he appeared at the radio station. He is given epithets like stoolie, gossip, traitor, national traitor, betrayer, and the back-stabbing engineer.

Bratt cooperated with a peace organization from the start but retained his anonymity. When he revealed his identity, the hero image was evidenced by the spontaneous public support given to him: "Many have called and supported what I did. I've gotten encouraging letters from all over Sweden." (p. 108) After a while, he was engaged to give a talk at the annual congress of the peace organization: "When I go up on the podium, the applause starts and goes on and on. I start to speak, but my voice fails – meeting over 100 people and feeling the waves of approval which wash over me is more than I can take." (p. 112) Another sign of being appreciated is that he was engaged to give lectures at different places in Sweden by political youth organizations and various church organizations. As an example of the reactions he received: "After the lecture a woman comes up to me. I admire you more than I can say for what you did, she says with tears in her eyes and gives me a hug." (p. 122)

After Bratt had talked at a church meeting, the minister said in his sermon:

> "This morning I had a pretty good idea of what my sermon would be about. But then Ingvar Bratt came and ruined everything," he began. A smile goes round the congregation. Then he talks about our tendency

to feel little when we hear about people who have done something big."
(p. 136)

Against this background, it is only natural that Bratt himself makes the following reflection: "Through the reactions I meet all over the country I have begun to realize that I am carrying not only the yoke of the traitor but also the wreath of the hero." (p. 135)

Further evidence of this heroic aspect is that a film is being prepared about him and that people still call or write to him for support. They relate their own fights against employers or about how they, too, wished they had the courage to "speak up." Several formulate his impact on them as revelations: "We want you to know that many of us have woken up because of what you've done. We are so very grateful." (p. 145)

Ingvar Bratt was never formally punished, since no law covered his behavior.[6] Neither did he lose his job since the laws on employment security in Sweden severely restrict firing people.[7] Not only did he escape formal sanctions, but Bofors' name was so smeared in the press that the new managers tried to alter the negative image by publicly thanking Bratt and informing all their employees that he had made a good contribution. (*Expressen* /Swedish daily/ February 8, 1988)

The Case of Stanley Adams

Other revealers might not be so lucky in achieving a hero image but can still leave a nimbus of "the good man" behind them. Stanley Adams seems to better fit the image of the martyr.[8] He was not hailed as Bratt was, or at least not while the affair, caused by his revelations, lasted. Afterwards he was helped and taken care of; but that is the fate of martyrs, not heroes. His revelations concerned Roche, the Swiss medical company, and its illegal business transactions: they were involved in a cartel directed against the third world's medical market. Adams reported this to The European Commission and one staff member revealed his name to Roche. Adams was imprisoned in Switzerland for treason and industrial espionage.[9] His wife committed suicide while he was in prison. He was then left alone with three small children; and he tried, after a while, to build a new life in Italy. His plans were thwarted because of his imprisonment, however, since the banks were no longer prepared to support his new business. A few years later he further destroyed his chances of building a future in Italy by testifying against Roche on the Seveso scandal[10] and by stating that Roche had had secret, perhaps illegal, connections with Christian Democratic politicians. After this he was blacklisted. Not only were loans totally blocked and permits or licenses difficult to obtain, but he also found it difficult to just get a job.

His book, *Roche versus Adams*, starts with the description of a wealthy, successful, happily married man, and continues, after the revelations, with a seemingly endless report of struggles, some of them against the machinery of justice and others to pay back the loans he took to start a farming business. He could not pay since he was unable to start the farm. He was again imprisoned for a while for failure to pay his debts, and was threatened with a new term of imprisonment in connection with a bankruptcy. The European Commission failed to help him, and he had to rely constantly on friends for last-minute financial help. He stayed in Italy for six years, where for long periods he could not afford to support his children, but had to leave them with relatives and friends. One option he had was to go to friends in England who were prepared to help him get a new job. However, since he had big debts in Italy he was not permitted to leave until they were paid.

With all of his problems, it is no wonder he touches on the martyr-theme himself: "I never set out to be a martyr. I never wanted to suffer for any cause. All I ever intended to do was pass information quietly. . . ." (p. 221)

Other evidence of his martyrdom is the type of mobilization the affair produced. This seemed to be directed more toward helping him and to start discussions of civil rights and about the responsibility of the European Commission, than to correcting the wrong-doings of Roche. A committee, The Appeal Committee, was organized on his behalf. A television film was made about him, after which people wrote encouraging letters and sometimes included monetary contributions. (pp. 165–167) Ernest Glinne, a Belgian member of the European Parliament, wrote an article where he described Adams as the Dreyfus of Europe. (p. 227)

He was finally able to leave Italy and build a new future in Britain. However, during the whole period of the affair (the revelation took place in 1973 and the book was written in 1984), he was never portrayed as a champion of the original cause against bad business practice concerning medicine or chemicals. He did not come to be used as a symbol for a cause, as Bratt did.[11] Nor did he seem to have achieved an image as a champion for health rights. He did not turn into an Ellsberg or a Ralph Nader because he was not attached to a group, and he did not have a platform for the cause when he initially leaked the information. Furthermore, he was "discovered" after he had already suffered, thereby giving him the title of martyr instead of before, when he could have been called a hero, fighting courageously for what is right. Possibly the cause (medical companies' business manipulations) at the time had not been sufficiently articulated or clear-cut for a popular collective to be formed around it.

Even revealers of commonly defined dirty secrets do not automatically gain a hero or martyr status for a cause. Some, as Serpico, can rather be described as "lonely crusaders."

The Case of Frank Serpico

Frank Serpico is described in Maas's (1973) book as an idealistic young policeman who fought against corruption in the police force. Ever since childhood, he had dreamed of becoming a police officer. Not only did policemen command respect and carry prestige in his neighborhood, but they acted as arbitrators in conflicts. His image of policemen was that they were "tough but fair." When he graduated from the Police Academy, he believed every word of the importance of being a good public servant in the speeches held at the ceremony. (pp. 44–45, 55)

When, as a police officer, he encountered a "small-type" corruption such as policemen not paying at restaurants, etc., he solved it by not accepting free meals himself. As a plainclothesman, he first tried to "do his own thing", and dissociated himself from his colleagues when they took bribes. By not accepting full membership in the We, he posed a danger to the other policemen, who subsequently reported him anonymously for a minor wrongdoing. Angered by this, he took his first step on his career as the exposer of police corruption. (pp. 126–127)[12]

After several years of attempts to change the system by informing various superiors, he finally informed the media. (p. 255) When the mayor's press secretary heard about this, he decided to ". . . beat *The Times* to the punch." (p. 256) The Knapp Commission began with public, televised hearings. A few policemen were indicted but nothing more happened. Serpico left his job after being shot and wounded (rumor had it that he was set up by his colleagues), and was granted a disability pension.

Serpico, of course, could not be formally punished for his disclosures. The police department was put in a difficult position – the high-ranking officers had to look as if they were concerned by corruption while simultaneously not wanting its existence to become public knowledge.

Nor did Serpico get a platform outside the police from which to work for this goal. In the book, *Serpico*, one does not read about him being praised, or sought-after, or being a celebrity. He got support and respect from a few other policemen and some lawyers, however, and he commanded the attention of the media – a book was written about him. The two groups or collectives that he could be said to be working for were "the public" and the "honest cops." The "honest cop" group is a problematic "back-up" group since it already exists in the We by trying to protect itself and by shielding its secrets. The public is problematic in another way: it constitutes a too amorphous and unorganized collection of people to form a supportive group. Serpico thus lacked the equivalent of Bratt's peace organizations or the health organizations, which could have been a potential platform for Adams, to rally to his cause. It is no coincidence that his fate was different from Bratt's and Adams's. One can not gain a hero or martyr image by oneself, others are needed to define you as such. Even if Serpico finally got a lot of attention and was admired by some, he can rather be portrayed as a lonely crusader, who fights in spite of not receiving support.

A Parenthesis - The Process of Becoming a Confirmed Whistle-Blower

All three of those described above had initially only planned to reveal what they thought of as wrong in order to correct it, and then to continue their lives quietly without having their identity revealed. The mere fact that books were published about all three of them is evidence that this did not happen. As Becker (1960) has shown, the road towards commitment is often crossed by what he calls *side-bets*. That is, our commitment is usually not a product of a ready-made goal, but of a process made up by coincidences and nonplanned effects of our behavior which lead to further activities that step-by-step strengthen our commitment. Even if the initial goal of the revealers was simple – to correct a wrong – reality intervened, changing the situations for the revealers. When their revelations became known, their information and identity became public property. Sometimes interested parties demanded more when the revealers were hesitant. Sometimes the actions of their enemies or counterparts served to strengthen their determination.

All of them had to pay a price for going against their We. Thus, they had to make these costs meaningful. In a sense these can be interpreted as social and emotional investments that cannot be ignored or discarded. Adams' wife took her life. If he stopped fighting, her suicide would be meaningless and not worth anything.

Stanley Adams can be used to further illustrate the above. First is his description of the situation just before he was arrested for having turned over his information: "As far as I was concerned, my part in the case was over. I had left Roche, I had done what I felt was right, and I had no further involvement. In the spring of 1974 my family and I had left Switzerland and moved to Italy. . . . I was immersed in the practicalities of developing a large industrial pig farm." (p. 42) Ten years later, after endless struggles, the affair *was* his life, and it had taken on a meaning beyond itself. He writes, as his last comment in the book, after stating that he will continue his fight:

How, I do not know, but I will do it. And I shall do it not only for me, but for all those other potential whistle-blowers who now look at me and think, as they are meant to think, "It's not worth it," and keep silent. Because we need them. The world needs them if it is to survive. The fiercer the pressures to keep silent, the more urgent the need for people to speak out. (p. 228)

Stanley Adams saw himself as a potential *model* for others. Interestingly enough, such models were also evident in Bratt's book. Perhaps it is especially important for those who go against their We to have such "reference individuals." Bratt actually wrote about Adams, for example. His comments after viewing the television film made on Adams shows that this did not work as an elevating experience. Due to the tragic air surrounding the Adams's case, it rather depressed him – but perhaps strengthened his anger towards the establishment that both of them fought against. The American revealer Daniel Ellsberg seems to function as a "hero for the heroes," however. He was characterized in a newspaper article as the "father figure for all revealers" in a report from a Swedish symposium on civil courage, where he received a prize together with Ingvar Bratt. (*Sydsvenska Dagbladet* /Swedish daily/ June 14, 1988, p. 4)

Betrayers as Social types

So far the possibilities of different groups seeing one and the same person in different and incompatible roles have been analyzed. The discussion has been focused on the role of the revealers. These are people often clearly seen as good from one perspective and just as clearly bad from another. Other social types of betrayers as collaborators inhabit roles that may be more mixed. Therefore there is some leeway when judging their good- or badness. Such labeling seems to rest upon deciding or judging their motives. Interestingly enough, in some cases, as we have seen by the book titles in the beginning of this chapter, this issue can catch the imagination long after the actions took place.

It should perhaps be added in this context that attributed motives were not discussed concerning the revealers since their nobleness is, so to speak, built in. To judge from a review of books on revealers, noble motives are a necessary condition – otherwise one does not qualify as a whistleblower: " . . . this reader would have liked more emphasis on the difficulties of distinguishing whistleblowing from other activities – those of the paranoid, of the difficult employee, or ostensible resisters masking their own culpabilities, and so on." (Golembiewski 1989, 93) This is one of the illustrations of the importance of moral evaluation as to betrayal, discussed elsewhere in this book where the act may be the same but the outcome in definition of act and actor varies.[13]

However, if one wants to present a typology for betrayers in general as social types, it should include the dimensions of the presence or absence of attributed "noble motive" and, as above, of "supporting group." Since it is the image of betrayers, not whether betrayers do have noble motives, it is the attribution of motives that is important. The archetypical collaborator Quisling has, for example, been described as a noncorrupted, ascetic, religious man who was sincere in believing that he was the protector of his people. (Hayes 1971; Littlejohn 1972) The genus "quisling" is evidence of this not being an accepted image of the collaborator. It goes without saying that the supporting group has to be powerful or influential enough to make its definition count. A typology of betrayers, according to the potential for a "moral doubleness" of good and bad could thus be formulated like this:

	Supporting Group Behind	
Attributed noble motives	Yes	No
Yes	1	3
No	2	4

1. betrayer/heroes.
2. betrayer/martyrs, lonely crusaders.
3. batrayers/unintended benefactors
4. betrayers/betrayers.

Type 1 and 2 have been discussed above. Apart from whistleblowers, one may also be include informers or spies in some specific contexts, as in a war, in type 1. Some of the witnesses during the McCarthy era also aquired a somewhat glorious image, as discussed in chapter 2. Type 3 are those who betray for greed, power, or the like; and while the supporting party may recognize this fact, the betrayal will benefit them since they have a common enemy. An example would be one of the super powers supporting a guerrilla group seen as traitors from the point of view of their country. The support could be given in spite of recognizing that the guerrillas were organized by power-hungry old tyrants, but one may share the hopes of overthrowing the sitting regime. (When support is given in such cases, attempts will probably be made to find noble traits and in polishing their image.) When I first started to experiment with this typology, I saw a further example for type 3 in betrayers/professionals. For example this would have included professional spies. These, however, are from the beginning entrenched in Them, thus even when pretending to be members of a We, they are not "betrayers."[14] (Philby and other such spies are not classified as "professionals.") Type 4 includes betrayers who are thought to betray because of non-idealistic reasons, all the while simultanously not being able to lean on a supporting group (as this means more than simple protecting). Such betrayers may be helped and protected but not glorified by their employers. Concrete examples are the tattle-tale, the police informer, the scab, and the collaborator.

A typology of this kind may hopefully point to some of the distinctive features in the labeling of betrayers. Typologies are however necessarily schematic. Real life makes attributions less one-dimensional. The case of spies shows how attributions can vary. A few, like Philby, may be hailed by those who use their betrayals. Others will neither be protected nor hailed by their masters. Furthermore, if one looks at some collaboraters' images as they develop historically, the verdict of their actions seems dependent on their attributed motives. One writer compares two well-known collaborators in this manner: "Laval collaborated with the Germans in order to cheat them, Quisling in order to assist them." (Littlejohn 1972, 51) Even though Laval was sentenced to death as a traitor and later historians have been – as with Pétain – more sympathetic in their designations, Laval does not fit the martyr image. Still, Laval and Pétain are not the simple betrayers they used to be.

In conclusion, it might not suffice merely to state with a sociological cliché that calling a betrayer a hero is simply a matter of perspective. Some have little or no chance of ever being portrayed as heroes. Those not joining a strike, "scabs," or police informers, are such types of betrayers. Even if they themselves have noble motives, it is difficult to formulate these reasons so that they appear to others in the same manner. Furthermore, they have no collective or group behind them who could rally to such claims of ideals. Regarding scabs, for example, employers may well protect them, but they do not praise them. Apart from the absence of a glorious cause, openly praising them would certainly antagonize strikers, and negotiations would be made more difficult. Nor can scabs, police informers, or collaborators ever belong to the other side: the employers, the police, or the enemy. The betrayers who do not have opportunities of also being given a glorious status are those not given membership in another We.

Notes

1. Perhaps "formal" is not the salient feature, but lacking a better concept I use it since it indicates the possibility of a heavy sanction that furthermore can be applied with the full force of the state.
2. The cases have been chosen so that they will illustrate the differences, that is, I have not made a systematic or thorough study of revealers. Daniel Ellsberg, who would be a hero in the typology, for example, is not included since I have a better knowledge of Ingvar Bratt. For the sake of brevity I have chosen only one example of each type.
3. As to Bratt's story, I have also collected articles in newspapers about his case. Regarding Adams I have interviewed his Swedish publisher and a journalist who met him when he was visiting Sweden. The only material on Serpico, however, is Maas's book.
4. Not surprisingly, there were many speculations surrounding the death of this official as to whether it was murder rather than the suicide it was claimed to be.
5. The quotes, all taken from Bratt's book, are translated from the Swedish.
6. Some time afterwards a law was suggested to the Parliament, popularly called "Lex Bratt," which was meant to restrict the legal possiblities of employees to inform outsiders about their companies.
7. He did leave his old job but this was due to informal reasons because he wanted to stop working with weapons and because of the climate at the old working place, as his revelations were not greatly appreciated.
8. The "martyrdom" may, of course, as many social typings, be temporary. According to his Swedish publisher, Adams was said to be leading a rather content, quiet life at present, having got a fairly good position at a university partly due to his revelations.
9. He was sentenced under articles 162 and 273 of the Swiss penal law. Article 162 concerns crimes against business secrets, article 273 crimes against the state. Adams was accused of stealing economic information and handing it over to a foreign power. According to Adams, this is a rare type of law; only South Korea and South Africa have comparable ones. (Adams, pp. 49)
10. On July 10, 1976, a factory exploded in Seveso. The town was covered by a gas cloud containing the very dangerous poison dioxin. The company had not reported that they handled this substance and had furthermore failed to plan for emergency measures in case of an accident. The scandal included the authorities since they had failed to inspect and instruct the company to organize relevant safety measures.

11. According to his Swedish publisher an organization called Health Action International took care of him for some time after he moved to Britain, but this is quite different from being its symbol or champion.
12. This is one of many illustrations of betrayal creating betrayal – a theme discussed by Luhmann (1979) in the more general terms of distrust breeding distrust.
13. Even though the moral evaluation of "whistleblowers" in this sense is unproblematic, it is still important for them to consider their own motives as "pure." Bratt does a lot of soul-searching in his book concerning his "real" motives.
14. See, for example, the distinction made by agents of the British Secret Service as reported in Spycatcher (Wright 1987, 136) between traitors and professional spies – the former having been in the We, while the latter, even if pretending to be members of the We, are identified as belonging to Them. See also the discussion in chapter 2 on "misplaced confidence."

4

Neutrality as Betrayal

Even though the label betrayer has been affixed, the situation can act as a positive or negative modifier as discussed in the previous chapter. However, one may look at the problem from a reverse angle and examine how the situation may create betrayers. Sometimes pointing towards a betrayer can be used in an awkward situation; the convenient explanation of why things went wrong. In certain social contexts betrayer roles are always evident, they are there to be filled – in prison, there is the role of the rat; in school, the tattletale or the snitch; in war, the traitor. Here however, I want to examine how situations can create more ambiguous roles liable to be associated with betrayal. The roles discussed are all characterized by being middle positions.

In times of conflict, it is commonly believed that linear grouping occurs – two camps on opposing sides accompanied by some strays in the middle. The social forces circumscribing such middle-of-the-roaders is the object of this chapter. Put another way, the idea of being neutral, as is wellknown sociologically, is not simply making a declaration to that extent without involvement.[1] Each camp obviously tries to win you over. Moreover, in many conflicts, there is a moral demand for you to choose sides: "Take a stand!", " Have an opinion!" Recognizing these social forces is important in a discussion of betrayal because if you insist on remaining neutral, you may not only be accused of indifference – the risk is greater; namely, that you will be cast in the role of betrayer.

Middle Positions Associated with Betrayal

Some forms of neutrality or positions in the middle that risk being identified with betrayal will be discussed and compared to one, the mediator, that does not. The first position is that of the nonparticipation in a taken-for-granted, good cause, i.e., the failure to join a crusade. The second variant are those who, during a conflict, declare the We/Them conflict irrelevant. The third is held by those who formally declare that they are neutral but are believed to have taken this position out of convenience. A fourth type includes people who cooperate or negotiate with the enemy while the more righteous demand a stricter noninvolvement or open conflict. A fifth variant consists of those performing in roles that demand objectivity: researchers, diplomats, etc., and in their reporting present facts that should not be revealed.

* * * * *

In Whyte's classic study *Street Corner Society*, a study of an Italian slum district, a nice illustration is provided of the first type of forbidden neutrality. A local election created a social climate at a settlement house for the unemployed, which caused neutrality to be equated with betrayal, even though neutrality was officially encouraged. The election stood between Wickman and Murphy. Wickman, who was supported by those running the settlement, was a man with inherited wealth and high social status. He was considered by his admirers as "clean," nice, and as having an excellent character. The other candidate, Murphy, was thought of as crooked and corrupt, a man who had made his money in politics. He was, however, the man of the people. Whyte described the following incident:

> One afternoon I was standing with Nutsy and several other corner boys when a young Italian who taught art classes in the Norton Street Settlement approached us on his way to the house. The corner boys noticed that he was wearing a Wickham button on his lapel, and they engaged him in an argument. The art teacher was distinctly on the defensive and claimed only that this was a free country, that he was not bothering the corner boys, and that he had a right to vote as he pleased. To this, Nutsy gibed, "You're just a yes-man!" "Sure I'm a yes-man," the man answered. "I have to be. My bread and butter depends on it." (1973, 100)

Whyte commented on the situation as follows: "It was the general rule for the Settlement to remain neutral in politics, but somehow this was thought to be different from other campaigns. It was a struggle between good and evil. In such a contest there could be no neutrality." (1973, 100–101)

Another case where an issue is considered so self-evidently good that no neutrality can be allowed is that of branding informers in prison. According to those I interviewed, it was necessary to join the denouncers of informers. Not only was it forbidden to be friendly with snitches but remaining neutral or behaving indifferently was almost as bad. By failing to join the crusade one risked being cast as a snitch oneself. (See chapter 6.)

Thus in situations where the social pressure stems from the fact that the issue is considered so unequivocally correct if you do not take part in the actions of the We, you will be labeled a betrayer of the just cause. If one insists on not taking part in the "right" line in cases as described above, one probably has strong motives for this. The inmates not concerned with snitch-hunting reported that they did not care enough anymore. Some stated this with regret – the criminal group and their identity as criminals were not as important as they had been. In these cases one had more or less left the We. In other cases the reasons were more instrumental: one did not wish to risk a longer sentence if caught punishing informers.

* * * * *

The reasons for nonagreement may not always be so defensive. Those who abstain for reasons of ideological inclination may appear more threatening. One might have been part of a conflict and suddenly see it in a different light – here it may be the conflict *per se* that is seen as irrelevant. To change the definition of the situation in such a manner can be as bad as joining the enemy – an act of pure treachery. An illustration of this was given by the acts of the Protestant army in Ireland, the UDA (Ulster Defence Association). One of its fighters had begun to question the cause of the fight. He had declared that the real enemy was poverty, not the Catholics; and this was an enemy common to both poor Protestants and poor Catholics. The dangerous message he brought was obviously that the old We/**Them** was not relevant and that the long-lasting fight where so many were sacrificed was not significant. Moreover, some young men were said to have been taken in by the argument. No wonder he was shot as a traitor.[2]

* * * * *

A third type of neutrals are those who publicly declare themselves as such while the surrounding world knows they are not. They are those who are believed to hold the middle ground just for the sake of convenience. Those who believe that the neutrals are really on their side thus see them as betrayers who do not dare to join the fight. In this case, apparently, it is thought that the term neutral is held up as a shield that one is hiding behind – "Everybody should be allowed to be neutral." or: "One has no moral obligation to join a fight." Sometimes the legitimation is more "aggressive," so that neutrality acquires a value of its own.[3]

As a Swede, for example, one still risks being treated contemptuously by one's Nordic neighbors because Sweden was neutral during World War II while they were not. I believe the contempt is based on two elements. First of all, the role of the neutral in such a conflict forces one to act impartially – this involves giving the enemy some concessions. The resentment toward Sweden stems partly from such actions. For example, the Germans were permitted to bring soldiers by train through Sweden, the so-called "transit trains," from Norway to Germany and from Germany to Finland. Furthermore, Sweden exported ore to the weapon manufacturer Krupp in Germany. The resentment also involves an accusation of letting others suffer and do the fighting, that is, not only getting off the hook but letting the others foot one's moral bill.[4]

Another example of this type of unglorious neutrality is one that a friend told me about that involved a conflict at her workplace. The conflict had split the office in two camps, with some trying to remain neutral. During an intense period with a strategic decision having to be made, my friend tried to talk one of the neutrals into taking an open stance since he had informally admitted being drawn to her camp. He had previously declared that he did not want to choose sides because he hated fights and he wanted to remain friendly with everyone. Now she said this issue could quite probably be important for him, too, in the future and he was the one who could tip the scale. When he still refused she stormed out, slamming the door and screaming, "He who has no enemies, has no friends."

* * * * *

The fourth group consists of those who deal with the enemy – that is, those who do not hold the lines properly.[5] Such people are sometimes labeled "collaborators." The issue can revolve around the question of whether one should negotiate or not. Here the debate might be conducted between the soft- versus the hard-liners. In such a position those willing to negotiate or to compromise can be seen as "selling out." Another example is the situation when the fight is more or less settled and the enemy is in power. Now, one can fight against all odds or employ some form of passive resistance. Both of these are somewhat honorable since in both cases one takes a clear stand. But the third, working with the enemy even if not for his cause, is definitely questionable. Because, if you agree to this, your hands are apt to become dirty – you will have to enforce at least some of his decisions; and you will have entered into a relation that leaves little room for resistance. Hence the criticism against those who accept or stay on in administrative positions during a war. These objections are illustrated in the harsh treatment by Blacks toward other Blacks who have accepted positions as mayors in the new homelands in South Africa.[6]

Other examples can be drawn from World War II. In a book about the retribution in Denmark, the author discussed the criticism against those who collaborated. Many of those who did it were accepted afterwards and their claim of acting for the best of society was accepted. But accepting such a position could be fateful. A vital factor seems to have been whether one had a social base ready to join one's defense. Tamm, the author, discusses a Gunnar Larsen who was branded as a traitor to his country:

> ... Gunnar Larsen was a victim of the policy of negotiation that he had represented. As an unpolitical minister, he got no support from his colleagues, and his background in "big business" made him a given prey for those who through the retribution movement wanted to smash exactly that group. (Tamm 1985, 481; my translation)

* * * * *

The fifth variation that will be discussed here is the branding of those who do not take a stance because they are cast in a role that demands objectivity. Good spies and diplomats are supposed to report on facts, not on wished-for conditions, to their employers. The reason for this is obviously that this is the most effective for the employers when making decisions. This can be a risky business. An indicator of the unpopularity of those dedicated to do a good job is the fact that in totalitarian countries, spies are said more often to report what their bosses want to hear. (Berger 1963, 6) Even in open societies the truth is not always welcome:

> Suspicion of diplomats by strong heads of government is a common trait. An official of America's State Department complains that whenever she explains to the White House how another country will react to an American policy, she is accused of taking the foreigner's side. (*The Economist*, July 16, 1988, p. 28)

Researchers are another group whose role requires objectivity in the presenting of facts. Still, social scientists may be expected not to reveal unattractive facts about so-called underdog groups. A study of Black pimps provoked the following reactions:

> When Christina presented a paper on pimps a few years ago at the American Anthropological Association meetings in San Diego, one Black professor walked out of the room saying he was "sick to his stomach." Another Black academic, a young lady, took a militant stance and argued that the study should never had been made. "White people have been telling Black people for years that they're nothing but a bunch of pimps and prostitutes," she said, "and we don't need a study like this. Why don't you study some of your disgusting White suburban wife-swappers?" (Milner and Milner 1972, 11)

The authors were arguably not real betrayers because they were not Black middle-class people themselves. However they may have qualified (as belonging to a We that is betrayable) in their accusers' view purely as anthropologists – as having, I believe, as sociologists, a tradition, identity, and image as liberals working for civil group causes. Moreover, they may in their accusers' view have overstepped the ethical lines in reporting about a group they had gained access to through trust.[7]

The sensitivity of reporting as accurately as possible exists because while doing this one may present unwanted images of the We or destroy a commonly held definition of a situation or an image of a group. Diplomats might disrupt the image of the enemy by making them appear less like enemies. They may do this by explaining the other side's ideas and actions and thereby make their views seem more rational. Others may destroy an image by a group supposed to be protected by the We (thereby half belonging to the We, a sort of relative to the We) by reporting facts that should be covered up.

A Contrast – The Mediator

Roles or positions that mean that one does not take a stance of unequivocal loyalty during a conflict to one's group is, as we have seen, liable to be interpreted as betrayal. There is, however, one role with such characteristics – a middle position during conflicts, that does not entail the danger of being stigmatized in this fashion – the mediator. A comparison between this role and those I have labeled neutral may be fruitful.

In order to do this, one can use the sociological classic, Georg Simmel's analysis of mediators in triads. (1964, 145–153) He believed that mediators come on the scene when there are no coalitions between conflicting parties because of opposing interests. The mediator, according to Simmel, becomes the whole group's representative and puts the collective interests above the private ones. It is possible for him to be impartial because he is above the conflict.

Impartiality does not necessarily mean as much as being considered a sincere "go-between", that is, one does not have to be free of ties to either side. In a commentary on the talks which changed Rhodesia into Zimbabwe and on the Camp David talks, it is said:

> In neither case was it important for the mediator to pretend to be impartial. At Lancaster House Britain openly jostled the guerillas (though everybody knew the British foreign ministry thought the whites ought to make peace). The Americans went to Camp David with a long record as Israel's close friend. . . . For the mediator evenhandedness does not much matter so long as both sides think he is a truthful go-between. (*The Economist* October 1, 1988, 63–64)

The mediator, then, is impartial; but above all he or she is a sincere go-between. In this the mediator clearly performs a positive function for both parties – something none of the "neutral-betrayers" are seen as doing. Furthermore, as opposed to those who refuse to take part in the conflict because it seems irrelevant for them, the mediator does care about the conflict. She or he takes it seriously and accepts its relevance. Neutrals of convenience also differ from mediators in that they are neutrals as a defense strategy while being thought of as really belonging to one of the parties. They are thus not playing a role in communicating different positions between the parties. For this they have no legitimacy. They share these characteristics with the collaborators. Collaborators exist furthermore in a position of subordination while the mediator is seen as being an independent actor. Those being demanded to report objectively sometimes report more than their employer wants but are still seen as belonging to a cause or an employer.

* * * * *

Different reasons for neutrals being cast as betrayers have been suggested above. However, one strong reason should not be omitted. Neutrality, middle positions, or the "we'll not take an open stand"-attitude are seen as weak positions. The step toward the enemy is considered closer from this position than if they were firmly entrenched in the We. In a book written by a woman who was active in the Belgian Resistance during World War II, the atmosphere in the beginning of the occupation is described:

The German authorities certainly fostered such a false sense of security, so that many burghers believed that their best reaction to the German presence was reluctant acceptance. From such a stance to open collaboration with the enemy was, for some individuals, but a short step. (Moszkiewiez 1987, 6)

Notes

1.   One example of this is the pressure to conform to the current values at any specific time, for example as discussed by Noelle-Neumann (1984).
2.   From Aktuellt, a television news program, March 17, 1988.
3.   See the discussion in Sweden on joining the European Community. Those who do not want to join use, among other arguments, that Sweden's neutrality would then become endangered. The projoiners look at this argument as an attempt of making "neutrality" sacred so that all discussions end when anyone uses it. (Cf. Bengt Lindroth, "Neutrality – our holiest cow", my translation. *Expressen* /Swedish daily/ December 27, 1988, p. 2.) This sacredness was interestingly interpreted in a debate about school books as being so strong that questioning Sweden's neutrality during World War II can be "slightly treasonable." (Radio debate, P1, September 22, 1989)
4.   For a harsh comment made by a Swede on Sweden's neutrality in a broader historical perspective, see Braconier (1989). It should also be added that I am not trying to present the entire picture – political scientists and politicians of that time would perhaps point to the advantages of Sweden being neutral as benefiting the other Nordic countries: a place to flee for their resistance, etc. Rather, I am giving the basic, emotional reactions to Sweden's role then.
5.   Here, drastic examples from war and similar situations are given, but many ordinary situations involving co-operation with Them, especially during conflicts or if they represent superiors, may be interpreted as akin to betrayed. The difficulties in becoming a foreman after having belonged to the collective of workers are related to this problem.
6.   This involves, of course, also the tensions between Blacks and "coloureds" who are admitted to and accept places in the South African Parliament. See, for example, Hugo's *Quislings or Realists – Documentary Study of Colored Politics in South Africa.*
7.   If this was the case, their informants did not agree since they did not see their business as something shameful.

5

Avoidance of Betrayal

Since betrayal is an ever-present possibility, steps are taken to avoid it. Individuals, groups, organizations, and states develop more or less intricate strategies in order to prevent an unwanted spreading of dangerous or embarrassing information. The main purpose of this chapter is to illustrate how common and basic such defenses are and how they are embedded in social life through habits, norms, and institutions.

The discussion below is organized so that first a few general social forces that function to reduce the possibility of betrayal are briefly presented. One such underlying influence is the fact that the act of betrayal is a shameful one and consequently has sanctions or strictures attached to it. This aura of shame also means that identity is at stake for the potential traitor. Furthermore, the fact that the act of betrayal is shameful causes parents, employers, etc., to teach the members of their We that sharing information is something one has to do with care. The social regulation for this can be seen in the socialization process. Finally, when secrets are shared, the situation *per se* can make for avoidance of betrayal: if one shares a secret, one create the possibility of extortion, thus reducing the willingness of any of the parties to divulge information.

Second, when underlying influences restricting betrayal are insufficient, actively worked-out and more precise strategies develop in social life to prevent the spreading of unwanted knowledge or to restrict information. Such strategies are worked out by individuals or groups, which is not to say that they have to be consciously applied. It may be done on a routine basis. Naturally, one such preventive strategy is the use of silence. Since this is so basic I have discussed it in its own right. Besides the strategy of silence, there are others restricting information. For analytical purposes I have divided these strategies into those applied to guard or hinder one from revealing things oneself, and another group of strategies used to keep others in line.

The fact that the third party, that is, those who superficially would seem to benefit from a betrayal, may help to suppress it will also be discussed. Finally, actors' negotiations concerning betrayal versus nonbetrayal will be commented on.

General Social Forces Reducing Betrayal

One basic social attitude toward betraying is that it is a shameful act – in some contexts, even a crime. This implies that there are sanctions attached to it. Therefore, one of the most basic deterrents could be the knowledge that the act of betrayal can result in punishment. Social control at work is evident all the way from the level of formal groups where sanctions are stated in the law to that of informal punishments in informal groups.[1] States try to keep their vital secrets by applying stiff, often the stiffest, punishments for treason. Informal sanctions can range from the extreme of some criminal groups where "ratting" can lead to assault or even murder to the more minimal sanction of school childrens making life unpleasant for a child who tattles.

Being a shameful act, we tend from an early age to teach the virtue of nonbetrayal; that is, the norm against snitching is often a vital part of any socialization. This task may be difficult since it clashes with demands for openness and honesty.[2] In some groups, this aspect of specialization is especially emphasized. Obviously criminals are taught on the street and in prison about the morality and the possible dangers in not being loyal. Prison inmates refer to this fact when explaining why snitching may never be excused. In most lawful occupations people are also taught about the wrongness in revealing what Hughes called "dirty knowledge." Sometimes this is advocated as "colleagueship." It is wellknown that policemen cover for each other to a large degree when one is accused. This loyalty not only arises from the solidarity originating at the workunit, but is part of their early teaching, according to Westley. (1956, 256)

Children are often left out when secret or sensitive information is communicated. In some situations, however, even children are welltrained in protecting information. A Black journalist from South Africa describes how she tried to get hold of the parents of Murphy Morobe, an activist in the United Democratic Front who had fled to the American Consulate. The parents lived in Soweto, which lacks street names.

Peter Magubane, the photographer, and I got lost. Some children looked at us suspiciously when we asked for directions. They swore that they'd never heard of a family called Morobe. Not until we met an acquaintance who could vouch for Peter and we showed them our presscards did they smile and point to a house a few meters away. (Vollenhoven, Sylvia. "In the home of the Morobes: There's a lot of money for paying the informer." *Expressen*/Swedish daily/September 18, 1988, p. 27)

Another consequence of betrayal being a shameful act is that of risking our identity. Being labeled a betrayer – a tattler, a snitch, an informer, a traitor – should be seen as a serious restricting force in its own right. This may appear threatening even after one has left the We. Many of the inmates I have interviewed in prisons or centers geared toward therapy or rehabilitation have, for this reason, often been very ambivalent on the subject of openness in therapy – no matter how "converted" they otherwise seemed to be.   Those with this attitude were even reluctant to be interviewed about the illegal aspects of prison life – selling drugs, violence, etc. Some said it was because they felt themselves to be "snitches" if they did, and these were men who planned never to return and who had lost all commitment to the criminal group.

A special form of deterrent is involved when both parties have "a hold on each other." This can also be seen as one general social force that prevents people from revealing to the outside, because they have mutually shared their dark knowledge. If only one party gives confidences, he or she will become a "psychological hostage" to the other. (Davis 1973, 112) In all probability this rarely happens, however, because confidences breed confidences and secrets are exchanged for secrets. This makes it less likely that either party will harm the other because in doing so, one will risk one's own secrets. In everyday life one probably seldom thinks consciously in such strategic ways, but I believe that the knowledge of "if I told about her confidences, mine would not be as secure" acts as an underlying restriction on telling.

The possibility of using extortion, however, might be limited. The actual use would not only destroy a relationship but would also turn the user into a betrayer. Take a case like the extramarital relationship. Both parties have been involved in something "naughty." They will share this if it gets out in the open, but he or she will also risk his identity as a man or woman of integrity.[3]

In a context such as the one described above, the implicit extortion is usually not stated. In other contexts such as during open conflicts or in dangerous situations where people are forced to act strategically, when both share harmful knowledge, extortion can be used quite openly. An example is given in Moszkiewiez's memoirs from her life as a member of the Belgian Resistance against the Germans. She feels threatened by one

of her own because she did not want to follow the actions recommended
by him:

At the time it seemed to me that Franz was beginning to assume some
Gestapo tactics and behavior of his own. My experiences of the last few
months had taught me that survival in this deadly game of secret
warfare meant forestalling the moves of friend and foe alike. I assured
Franz that he need not worry about me; I took his arm in mine,
comrade fashion, and looked him straight in the eye: "If they ever arrest
me, my dear, you may be sure that they will also arrest you. Don't
forget that we are in this together, for better or for worse."
(Moszkiewiez 1987, 75)

An "active way" of using extortion is to create a situation where this
becomes a possibility. The creation of such a situation can be said to be a
"betrayal insurance." Making someone an accomplice by sharing
compromising knowledge or behavior is one variant. Inmates in Swedish
prisons have told me about a tactic used when they have stayed in drug
rehabilitation centers. Newcomers who look like they could detect
forbidden drug use were taken to the side and offered drugs. If they
accepted, they shared the guilt and could not reveal what was going on.
This tactic might be a necessity when the issue centers on hindering a
betrayer from betray his new alliance. This is the case when he does not
betray because he wishes to enter a new We. A drastic illustration is
provided from the Nazi concentration camps that recruited Jews as
collaborators:

. . . collaborators who originate in the adversary camp, ex-enemies, are
untrustworthy by definition: they betrayed once and they can betray
again. It is not enough to relegate them to marginal tasks; the best way
to bind them is to burden them with guilt, cover them with blood,
compromise them as much as possible. They will thus have established
with their instigators the bond of complicity and will no longer be able
to turn back. (Levi 1988, 28)

Strategies Used to Prevent Betrayal

Apart from the general social forces or the situation *per se* (in shared
knowledge) that limit betrayal as described above, specific strategies are
applied to avoid treachery. The development of such strategies are, of
course, dependent on a whole range of facts and considerations. It would
appear that the more serious effects a betrayal might cause, the more

refined and elaborate strategies become. In some contexts one will find more emphasis on secrecy and tests of trustworthiness; while in other situations, they exist more or less routinely without much reflection. Classic illustrations of the former can be found in the spy literature; of the latter, in such everyday behavior as avoiding the known gossip.[4]

Discussed below are some examples of such strategies, which will be presented without claiming to be all-inclusive.

Silence

The use of silence will be discussed later as well, but first I want to deal with the theme by itself since it is such a basic mechanism for limiting the spread of harmful information.[5] The importance of silence is mirrored in the everyday life saying "silence is golden" that exists in most languages. (Holm 1951, 316) There are also warnings such as when one is reminded to "button one's lip" so that information is not spread by accident, or such as "even the walls have ears," and as a reminder that children are listening, "little pitchers have big ears."

Silence is advocated, I believe, not only to restrict information but also because once it is out in the open, statements have a more objective character – and are thus more difficult to deny. Not only is the difficulty of denial involved but we also tend to demand a permanency from each other – that is, we should not change our views.   If we do change our mind, even gradually, our friends might chide us with comments: "That's not what you said before!" or "That's not what you usually say." For politicians this is a problem that has to be taken into account, and solved.

> Seclusion was as important for the Camp David talks as the international spotlight was for Lancaster House. Cut off from the press (and from hardliners back home), the negotiators could say "what if?" to each other in between-session strolls. A leak could have destroyed an agreement. Since a position taken publicly is almost impossible to change, Mr. Carter let no one but his own spokesman anywhere near the press. (*The Economist*, October 1, 1988, 63)

The importance of silence is additionally reflected in the fact that many societies have regulated silence both as legal rights and as obligations.[6] Criminals have "the right to remain silent" when arrested to protect them from betraying themselves. Journalists have also "the right to remain silent" to protect themselves and their sources. Another group that has the same right is the police who, in some countries, can refuse to make the names of their informants public.

For some other groups the matter is formulated differently – they are obliged to remain silent in order to protect those who have given them information. Doctors, priests, lawyers, and social workers are cases in point where this obligation is formalized in law.[7] In other cases the obligation rests on informal understandings. The "service specialists" that Goffman discussed (1959, 153) often have professional ethics that oblige them to show discretion. Occupations of this sort, where individuals construct, maintain, or repair others' settings or personal fronts, make them knowledgeable about their clients' secrets without the latter learning corresponding secrets.

Furthermore, most occupations cannot be carried on without guilty knowledge. The knowledge is guilty, according to Hughes, in that " . . . it is knowledge that a layman would be obliged to reveal, or in that the withholding of it from the public or from authorities compromises the integrity of the man who so withholds it. . . ." (1984, 289) Therefore many people in various occupations are granted a "license" to obtain and keep secrets. In other words, using a dramatic example: if a layman heard a man confess to a murder, he would have to report it, while a Catholic priest hearing the same during a confession would not only have moral leeway but a moral duty not to tell. The license to keep secrets and the codes of ethics making service specialists keep their knowledge to themselves exists in order for such occupations to function at all. Our own profession, social science, would hardly be possible without it.

If the use of silence was uncomplicated and straightforward, it would not be so sociologically interesting. As it is, it is quite a feat to remain silent in the presence of others. We are required socially to talk; we speak, for example, of embarrassing or awkward situations when no one can find anything to say that will lighten up a situation. Not only are we required to talk to make a social encounter flow smoothly; but when it comes to secrets, we even have difficulties in not sharing them. (Simmel 1964, 333–334)

Even in situations where it is potentially detrimental to oneself to speak, some tend to talk anyway, as Aubert (1965, 296) has shown in relation to those in the Norwegian Resistance Movement during World War II. Even when our right to remain silent is regulated by law, it may be difficult not to talk. Hepworth and Turner note in their book *Confessions* that the legal right to remain silent collides with the social demand to talk. (1982, 141) They illustrate this by referring to a study of draft protesters who felt dutybound to justify their actions to FBI agents rather than use their right to remain silent. (Griffiths and Ayers 1967) The interrogation situation was interpreted as a social rather than a legal encounter since they were not able to isolate the demands from everyday expectations to talk. This was a rather special situation with idealistic young men involved. The same mechanism seems to be at work with ordinary criminals as well, however. Both they and the policemen I have interviewed report that inexperienced criminals are apt to "break" for the same reasons.[8]

When silence is mandatory, those demanding it often counteract our tendency to talk with some sort of ritual, exhortation, oral or written promise or codes that we agree to follow. The elaborate ceremonies concerning the oath of loyalty in secret societies are obviously designed to make an imprint on those swearing it. Even more routine, written promises of secrecy given by those working as interviewers, for example, have some of the desired effect – the function of this practice might be more to make an impact on the interviewers themselves than to constitute a solid legal document.[9]

"Telling Silence". The use of silence may be double-edged. Silence might betray or at least arouse the suspicion that there is something hidden that is damaging or embarrassing. This phenomenon is acknowledged with sayings like a "pregnant" or "revealing silence."[10]

In circumstances when talking or keeping quiet is a real issue and silence is a rational strategy, it might still be problematic. The inmates I interviewed all believed that silence during an interrogation was interpreted as guilt. They also believed that if the evidence was against them anyway, keeping silent could get them a stiffer sentence than if they talked as they might be considered uncooperative, a hardened criminal, or something of that sort by the court. This view was also shared by the policemen I interviewed – they claimed that this was an objective fact.

Attorneys who suddenly advise their clients not to talk during an interview may point out the things that were meant to be hidden, thus giving a clue to the interrogators:

Some information control actions may be taken in plain view, for example, when in the middle of an interview with an investigative agent the attorney tells his client to stop talking. Information control will be achieved by affecting the client's behavior, but its effectiveness is diminished because it communicates to the opposition that a sensitive point has been reached. In this situation, the government agent – his interest stimulated – is more likely to be able to force the defense attorney into substantive adversary argument about the legitimacy of nonresponse in the particular context. (Mann 1985, 8)

Since keeping silent may look suspicious, the refusal to talk may be used by those who want an answer. This strategy may be generally used both in everyday life and can be specific to some work experiences. Journalists use people's refusal to speak to press home their point by televising the person who says "no comment." This counter-strategy was reportedly also used in a social science study to make policemen talk. Questions in a questionnaire about whether a policeman would cover another in cases of illegalities such as stealing, or using unlawful violence, were formulated so that they: ". . . put the men on the hook because a refusal to answer *looked* incriminating. . . ." (Westley 1970, 112)

* * * * *

Now we will turn to a discussion of betrayal avoidance as individual tactics versus collective tactics. By individual tactics I mean those applied to guard oneself from betraying. Many strategies in the technical sense are, of course, the same; that is, for example, the destruction or concealment of incriminating written material. It is how and by whom they are learned and applied that seems sociologically interesting. Some of the techniques presented below will, therefore, be the same, but will be discussed separately from the individual actor's perspective on the one hand and from the collective's perspective on the other.

Controlling Oneself

An interesting variation of information restriction occurs when the individual deliberately acts so that he hinders or guards himself from betraying, since one has to take into account that not only others are untrustworthy but oneself as well. These self-controlling strategies are obviously not solely "made" by the individual but embedded in cultural recipes. Some ways in which the actor uses the particular self-discipline needed to avoid betrayal will be presented below.

(1) Avoiding through not telling. Sometimes self-discipline is spontaneous and is based on so-called tact, how we answer curious neighbors, too-nosy friends, etc., when we want to protect other neighbors or friends. We can pretend a lack of knowledge, or we can use outright lies if it becomes necessary. The extent to which these devices can be used in order to protect someone is, I presume, a matter both of personality and relationships. Lying to friends is no light affair – it certainly has a dampening effect on the friendship if the lie is discovered. In protecting

someone from a curious friend, we may end up as betrayers of the friend who asks. . . .

If it is not friends who ask the sensitive questions and hence an issue not quite as touchy, it may still appear rude not to answer. One way out is, therefore, to evade questions or to claim a lack of knowledge. Still, as most people are brought up in a culture that preaches the virtues of honesty, such evasions may embarrass people.

In some circumstances if, for example, one belongs to a collective pitted against another collective, one may enjoy sociopsychological support from one's own group when restricting information. This may occur even when one does not know the others in the We. The mere fact that one knows that others share the same situation may facilitate the suppression of information. One illustration of this is given in the memoirs of a girl in the Resistance when she reflects on her capacity for not telling even her closest friends and family about her involvement:

I definitely could not tell my parents the truth. The knowledge alone would have placed them in jeopardy. "Only those who can keep their mouths shut stand a chance of surviving," Jean had once told me. . . . I was duly impressed, but being by nature talkative, I found this secrecy very hard to bear. In retrospect I appreciate that my success in concealing my role in the underground owed a considerable amount to the fact that I knew of many boys and girls, some of them much younger than me, who worked for the Resistance and lived under the same difficult conditions. (Moszkiewiez 1987, 44)

Another group-support mechanism is that of anticipated reward or admiration from one's own group if one has been able to withstand the pressure to betray. To know, for example, that other inmates will welcome you warmly to prison must be important for those who have stoically kept quiet through months in jail. The contact-men, employers, and colleagues that spies and people in resistance movements have must fill the same function as potentially applauding "home audiences." Perhaps this type of recognition may even explain such dramatic refusals to betray as those refusing to give in under torture, even though they know they may die. They believe they will be remembered as someone who kept quiet in spite of . . . .

An interesting feature in the "not telling" strategy occurs when it involves not only the practice of not telling about the secret but not telling at all. This is done in order not to tell by mistake. In many police cases, for example, the evidence is not enough to convict someone. Therefore, both the policemen and criminals I have interviewed have attested that the most successful strategy during interrogation is to "clam up." This means that one refuses to talk, no matter what, in order not to give oneself or others away by lapses or contradictions. The logic behind an all-out refusal to speak is that such mistakes are easy to make once you start talking a little.[11] The same strategy can evidently be used by others in quite different situations. From Richardson's study of single women who had affairs with married men:

> Conversations with friends and family may be truncated as the single woman becomes more matter-of-fact and distant in her intentions, revealing little about her life for fear of revealing all (e.g. "I just repressed my life. I didn't talk about anything to anyone."). (1988, 216)

(2) Making sure of not knowing. Making sure of not knowing that which might be incriminating is common to people in some positions – politicians and hight-level management come easily to mind – when they want to reduce the risks for betraying or for being betrayed. Even if we are prepared to lie, it is always easier to deny knowledge if this fact is the truth. Few of us have effective poker faces and genuinely not knowing gives better "deniability." Furthermore, by not knowing, we reduce the psychological cost of keeping tabs on the things we are not supposed to know.[12]

The purpose for not wanting to know may be dual: to protect both oneself and others. Most superiors, for example, are responsible for the behavior of their subordinates at work. This means that if they learn about irregularities, they have to deal with them even if they do not want to. The superior, by avoiding unwanted information, can both be relieved of the duty to act and exonerated from possible forthcoming blame.[13] An illustration of this strategy was given in an article on the police. The sergeants in the study were friendly with their subordinates and did not like the station sergeant because of his harsh punishment of his men: "Thus, when problematic cases of rule-violation occurred, these sergeants didn't want to know. . . ." (Manning 1978, 86)

In some occupations one has a responsibility to pass on or to act on information about others, such as clients or colleagues, in a way that may be harmful to those people. In a study of American attorneys it is shown how keeping their clients from communicating too much information may be as important as obtaining information from them:

> Some attorneys, for instance, discourage the disclosure of facts that would negate a defense of lack of knowledge. They would not want to

find out that a client actually had knowledge of a fact that would prove criminal intent – knowledge of a report or the action of another person – if the government was also not going to find this out. The attorney can then more forcefully argue that the client did not know of the report or the action. (Mann 1985, 103)

(3) Avoiding conflicting positions – separating groups. One strategy in the area of nonbetrayal is to avoid belonging to more than one group simultaneously if the groups' interests might conflict in regard to an individual; in other words, so that one is not tempted or compelled to act in one group on information gained in the other group. During a study of a women's shelter, the issue arose as to how the members should deal with information women seeking help gave about illegalities: everything from tax evasions to children who were abused by their father. This problem became acute for those who in their ordinary work might meet the same women, possibly as clients. One social worker said, for instance, that even if a woman would not tell her about illegalities as a client, she would still have difficulties in ridding herself of the knowledge she already had acquired. She therefore left the shelter.

(4) Anonymizing the sources. When having to refer to a source in situations as diverse as in scientific publishing, in courts, etc., if one wants to protect the source, one must make this person as unidentifiable as possible. If one cannot conceal a source by giving it anonymity, one may "blur" it. This can be done, for example, by hinting at other possible sources, "throwing out red herrings."[14]

The police, whose reports are public, state that they at times protect those who give them information by formulating their reports as "it has come to the attention of the police that. . . ." This is done to protect both informers and common citizens afraid of giving evidence or appearing in court as witnesses. The Swedish police also use the so-called "public tips" telephone in this manner. The "public tips" telephone allows anyone to call anonymously and tip the police about illegalities. According to interviews with policemen, they sometimes claim tips had come from that source even if the information had in actuality come from criminals. They did so in situations where the source would otherwise be identifiable. Thus, while the manifest function of the "tips" telephone is to increase information from "concerned citizens," it also serves a latent one - to protect and camouflage police sources of informants.

Even when custom grants the right to maintain anonymity, sources may still be recognizable. This is the case when there are few sources known to have some specific information, or if the sources have unusual characteristics that are revealed in their statements. This is a problem that may appear in social science studies. In one of my studies, for example, I judged the anonymity to be insufficient.[15] The study was carried out in a small town and dealt with unemployed women. The material consisted of a questionnaire distributed to a large group and of a few in-depth interviews. In order to find some women to interview with the latter method, one of the staff at the unemployment office equipped me with names and addresses. These women were her case assignments, and she selected them so as to reflect as much diversity as possible. Because of this, the quotes I used would have been easily recognized by her. Even though this woman had promised to keep the names secret and honor the rules of confidentiality, and even though I judged her to be trustworthy, I nevertheless decided to inject a little uncertainty. This decision was also prompted by the nature of the interviews – some of the women admitted uses of the benefit system bordering on the illegal. Therefore, when I wrote the report, I claimed to have made more qualitative interviews than I actually had, and that I had chosen the others myself from the total list of unemployed women. Thus, to behave in what I judged to be an ethical manner, I was forced to make an unethical scientific report by falsely stating the bases of my qualitative material.[16]

(5) Avoiding incriminating signs. When We's need to remain secret toward the outer world and are simultanously composed of individuals unknown to each other, as are resistance groups during a war, the members need to be able to identify each other. Since they cannot do it openly, they have to employ some type of hidden signs. These have to be chosen with some care. The Belgian Resistance used, for example, membership cards when they started, but they soon changed to code words since the cards were too revealing when members were caught. (Moszkiewiez 1987)

In other contexts one may use the whole variety of impression management that Goffman has written about. If you are a spy working as a Western European diplomat, you avoid subscribing to communist newspapers if the Soviet Union is your real employer. Another revealing "sign" may be those you associate with. The same diplomat would avoid meeting Eastern friends unless the situation legitimized it.

Your membership in a group you wish to protect may also be concealed by publicly pronouncing different viewpoints than this group is known to espouse. In other words, it may be advantageous that acquaintances and others believe that one is a bit proenemy. Aubert (1965), who has analyzed the Norwegian Resistance in which he was a member during the World War II, noted:

It might sometimes be considered advantageous to appear slightly pro-German in relation to such people. For example, it was often reported, with genuine satisfaction within the organization, that some acquaintance had been led to believe that one was a rather weak patriot. (1965, 307)

A similar technique can be used in other secret situations, for example between an informer and his "employer." A prison officer told me in response to my inquiring about rewards for information:[17] "You know – an informer in a cell block – we're a lot harder on him – on the surface. It's really hell for him in the block (laughter). It's not a pretty game . . . but that's life."

Controlling Others – Group Strategies

Groups and collectives create different protective devices in order not to be betrayed. Some strategies are similar in content as those discussed above, but here they are viewed from the perspective of a collective.

(1) "Testing". One basic mechanism includes control of those persons they accept among themselves. In general, most relationships begin with "feelers" – confidences and secrets are held back until we know each other enough to trust neither party will betray the other. Luhmann describes the trust as a learning process that is not completed until we have had the opportunity to betray trust and have not used it. (1979, 44) Such opportunities may be provided by the potential trusters through different tests. These may, of course, be more or less elaborated; and they may for analytical purposes be divided in "before-trusting" and "after-trusting": before one accepts someone, and afterwards, when someone has aroused suspicions.

(1a) "Before-trusting". In some contexts testing takes on a more or less habitualized or ritualized form. If not ritualized, testing is at least habitually used in many occupations that require a team as the work unit, and where cheating and stealing (fiddling) are common. The English anthropologist Gerald Mars (1983) has studied such groups, and has made an elegant analysis of how their structure forms different recruitment, fiddles, and risks in getting caught. Tight work units, which he names "wolf-packs," (garbage collectors, dockers, printers, etc.) test their aspiring members outright if they do not know them beforehand.[18] One example of the testing was related by a garbage collector:

There are some old people who always leave two pence on the top of the dustbin. You'll always be careful emptying their bins, closing the gate, and so on. I suppose they [i.e., the rest of the dustcart crew] tested me at first; if I'd kept the two pences I wouldn't have lasted long. (1983, 89–90)

Another situation occurs in the workgroups that Mars has called "vultures." Here, one finds salesmen, truckdrivers, and waiters. They are not as tight as the "wolv-packs." They cooperate but they also compete. For them, more subtle mechanisms seem to be the line. Since most of them do not know that fiddling is part of their future job; and as breaking the law may not be inherent in their self-image, the trainers have to be careful. Salesmen teach the newcomer and test his receptivity for fiddling by showing him that it is necessary in their chosen occupation. Since the trainer does not know if the trainee is trustworthy, fiddling cannot be taught outright. Therefore, one jokes about it, hints around, and watches for signs that the new man has swallowed the bait. If not, the mentor can always back off by claiming: "I was just joking."

On regular rounds with myriad customers suggestions about adding a penny on here and there and advice on who to "watch out for" are made jokingly, as if only half-meant. At this stage they *are* only half-meant; if the trainee jibs at these suggestions, they can always be withdrawn and no harm is done. The joking tone, too, prevents suggestions being quoted against the trainer later on. (Mars 1983, 117)

(1b) "After-trusting". After information has been shared, suspicions may arise. In such a situation one may withdraw; but if this is not an option and determining reliability is crucial, one may decide to test reliability. One way of doing this is to plant information and then check whether it is passed on to undesirables. Such tests may be uncommon in everyday life[19] but among some groups such as criminals or in intelligence and police work, it is a well-known strategy. Their counterparts may also employ this method. In prison it is said that inmates plant information about illegalities to see whether a suspected fellow inmate reports them. One guard said that putting drugs in a particular place and telling the suspected betrayer about the place was one method used by inmates:

It can happen that a guard messes up when a thief has squealed about things up here and picked it up the same day they planted the stuff to see who the squealer is. Then the only thing you can do is get him out of there as fast as possible. 'Cause they've been testing him [the squealer] and set him up, and we found out too fast – yeah, then they know it's him. The two or three who were in the group . . . the two set up the trap and then sit back and wait, while the third swallow the bait. (Åkerström 1985b, 23)

(2) Restricting membership in numbers. Testing of various sorts are probably restricted to small groups, in big, bureaucratic organizations it would be difficult. In fact, the smallness of groups can be an advantage in guarding a group in its own right. For example, Lenin advocated restricting membership for this reason when training professional revolutionaries: ". . . the more we *restrict* the membership of this organization to persons who are engaged in revolution as a profession and who have been professionallly trained . . . the more difficult it will be to catch the organization. (Lenin 1929, 246)

(3) Separating groups. One effective device when restricting information is to minimize the possibility of transferring it to other competing groups. This can be done through controlling individuals' membership in such groups. Groups regulate this both in formal and informal ways. One of the reasons for informal norms discouraging association between opposing groups may be based on this wish for limiting access to vital information.[20] Examples of this is the "code" between criminals not to become friendly with guards.

Some occupations are characterized by the individual working with several groups or clients while none are able to control this individual fully. Occupations such as these are often entrepreneurial in kind. Mars calls such people "hawks" and has noted that they enjoy a statelessness. "In all these occupations . . . the hawk offers partial information, while keeping the complete picture of what is happening to himself." (1983, 55) The potential for double-dealing and treachery is obvious in such a situation. In order to protect individuals, groups, businesses, etc., formal rules are often employed to minimize the risk of someone using knowledge from one sphere to another in a harmful way. As an example, lawyers may not use information about one client against another.[21]

The mere possibility of destroying the reputation of a work place by working for employees with a conflict of interest is forbidden in the Swedish Law of Employment.[22] The employees at my university are informed about so-called conflicting sidelines: "The employee may not have employment or assignments or activities which can affect his or another employee's impartiality and loyalty in carrying out his duties or injure the reputation of the authorities." (*LUM*/monthly magazine issued by the University/ May 27, 1988, p. 2)

In other contexts the issue is not loyalty for instrumental reasons but the commitment *per se*. In the "greedy institutions" that Coser (1974) has written about, assurance of undivided loyalty can be gained by limiting or cutting off all the bonds to potentially competing social circles. The vanguard groups of political or religious movements have often operated in this way. The Jesuits, apart from being cut off from family, geographic homearea, etc., had no stable associates in the monastic order and could not aspire to episcopal staff. Thus they were denied all standing in organizations other than the Society. "Obedience . . . could be successfully inculcated to the degree that the typical Jesuit was removed from the influence of all competing foci of loyalties and allegiances and that the Society was his only reference group." (Coser 1974, 124) Similarly, the Bolshevik's method may be interpreted along the same lines: "The party attempted to monopolize the commitments of its members by cutting them off from all personal ties and obligations that might distract them from complete dedication to the tasks at hand."[23] (Coser 1974, 131)

(4) Social typings of unreliables. In groups and societies as a whole, typologies are developed as to who is reliable and who is not. Our society is generally in agreement that children and drunks, to name two examples, are "unreliables"; they are groups in relation to which one must use discretion regarding what should and should not be told.[24] Such people are judged potentially dangerous because they do not have restraints or judgment. Subgroups often have their specific division of reliables versus unreliables: ordinary thieves warn each other not to trust an addict. (Åkerström 1985:a, 1985:b)

Potentially unreliable persons are obviously all who share information. Those placed in a position where information is available while they simultaneously have less to lose than to gain, if pressured, are often considered "risks." If such people need not know, the group may discourage its members from revealing too much. Among the criminals I interviewed there was a rule, for example, of not telling wives or girlfriends. One reason for this was that the police could apply pressure by threatening to see to that their children were taken into custody.

Other typings are based on personal characteristics. Some people who are bitter or revengeful may reveal knowledge out of spite or for vengeance. The gossip might not "betray" but tell too much in order to talk for purely social reasons. Another related feature that may make for suspicion concerns people who are indiscriminatly sociable: too open and friendly by nature. The risk here would be that they lack discretion.

When someone arrives at a new workplace, neighborhood, etc., he might be warned about all such persons.

Dilemmas in Suspicion Awareness Contexts

In some contexts that Case (1987) refers to as "suspicion awareness contexts," information is dangerous to distribute even while still being vital for use in performing a task. Case studied racehorse trainers, who from the outside behaved in an irrational way. They did not give their jockeys all the possible information about the horses they rode. By restricting information in this way, they decreased the horse's chances of winning. At second glance, however, their behavior were not only rational but necessary. They had to guard their "business secrets" since the jockeys rode for other, rival trainers who were eager to collect any piece of information about other horses' strengths, weaknesses, and form. In this light the trainers' rules of "Never trust a jockey" made sense. Their dilemma thus consisted of:

> . . . revealing enough about his horse to bring victory and risk having it beaten in future races; versus telling little, hoping for success, and keeping the secrets of his horse to himself. . . . (Case 1987, 334)

Information that might prove damaging can also be restricted by organizational structuring. This, however, may have its own problems. In Aubert's analysis of the Resistance in Norway, several problems of secrecy are presented. One was due to the recruitment issue. Since one could not take on new members on ascriptive criteria; one recruited on the basis of trust. At times this meant friends or acquaintances. Such units that were based on chains of personal relationships were vulnerable, if one was caught, it was easy for the Germans to unravel the whole chain. (Aubert 1965, 290–291) Another dilemma in organizing restricted information in these contexts was the rule that ordinary members, apart from the leaders, only knew one or a few others. The fact that information was so differentially accessible coupled with an authoritarian structure enabled the leaders to manipulate members to a great extent. This was evidenced in the cases where *agent provocateurs* succeeded in becoming leaders. (Aubert 1965, 297) In Moszkiewiez's (1987) autobiography the same problem is described. During her time as an ordinary member in the Belgian Resistance, she never knew that she was employed by the British. She did not know because she had no direct channels to England due to security reasons. Or, rather, this was what her closest superior told her. However, he had his own reason for keeping her from talking to them: he turned out to be a double agent. Even when her suspicions of him grew, she could not air them as the channels to his superiors were closed.

Finally, a general problem of suspicion awareness contexts is, as Luhmann (1979) notes, that distrust breeds distrust. A drastic illustration of this process is described in an analysis made by a former prisoner in a Nazi concentration camp:

> The danger that spies and traitors would seriously threaten the whole existence of the prisoners was so great that one always took measures against possible treason. Many who came into contact with the SS's representatives without being initiated were in mortal danger. Only in a few, rare cases did one know already at the beginning what kind of contact it was and where it could lead – even against the individual's will. Some mistakes were made, which by itself is unforgivable, but which is comprehensible considering the difficult position . . . a few became "snitches" thanks to unfair persecution in the camp. Due to their desperation and lack of experience they saw no other way out than going over to the SS. . . (Kogon 1989, 259; my translation)

A general problem in social systems where distrust is emphasized is to establish "interpretations which allow the carrying out of distrusting *actions* but which explain away distrust as an *attitude*." (Luhmann 1979, 75)

The Surroundings Help . . .

The picture given above may be too one-dimensional. A situation is portrayed where two parties exist – one holds back information, while the other searches for it. Sometimes, however, those whom one would guess want information discourage the potential betrayer. The keeping of secrets may be a mutual operation – possible receivers of secrets may seemingly cooperate with those trying to guard them though not for the same reason.

Which mechanisms operate for such a mutual operation? One factor might be contempt, as discussed in chapter 2; but other mechanisms are at work as well. Wieder (1974), who studied staff and residents at a halfway house for addicts, has discussed how the code against snitching was used. He shows how the staff was able, by referring to the code, to deal with their own problems such as explaining why therapy did not work or why the place was not "clean" (i.e., free from drugs). One could also prevent proposals for new activities because one would argue that these would not work because of the code. Furthermore:

. . . "telling the code" also relieved staff members of much of their responsibility to be knowledgeable about the affairs of specific residents, since the code provided for prohibitions against a resident's confessing to staff and against a resident's informing staff about the affairs of other residents. (Wieder 1974, 162)

The same mechanism might well be at work in other workplaces, such as day-care centers and schools. Sometimes even when a parent is aware of his offspring's misdoings, he is relieved if he is not informed since this would mean that he would have to act.

Another restraining mechanism in Wieder's study is empathy with the potential snitch:

PA: If Gonzales [one of his cases] came in here and started blabbing about somebody in such a way that other people would know about it, I'd be concerned for him. I would try to prevent him from doing that.
W: Why?
PA: Because I have a concern for him. I wouldn't want anybody killing him.
(Wieder 1974, 162; W stands for Wieder and PA is one of the staff, my comment)[25]

This mechanism is also possible to transfer to other contexts. Parents would not wish their children to suffer the reputation of being known as tattlers (even if the consequences can't be compared with the above). Perhaps this is the strongest reason for teaching children not to inform, even if one had earlier taught them to be honest. . . .

Negotiating

Different "moralities" concerning betrayal may come into conflict with each other. Sometimes they are easy to solve. If I study criminals and find out about some petty illegalities, I would certainly place my promise of confidentiality to my informants in the forefront.

At other times the situation is more difficult and conflicting ethics are at stake. Such a situation is recounted by Peterson (1984). The issue was whether the identity of "sloppy" forensic laboratories should be revealed even though the research team had granted them anonymity. The funding agency thought the facts should be revealed whereas the advisory committee guiding the project said no. Apart from several procedural and instrumental arguments (such as "will we get further funding if we refuse?"), some "pure" ethical dilemmas arose: should one keep the promise of anonymity versus whether the "sloppy" laboratories should be identified in the interests of justice and the public, especially considering that people could be acquitted or sentenced on forensic evidence. (The problem was solved by compromising: the identifying codes were not destroyed but were handed over to the directors of the laboratories. This action was then communicated to the interested parties.)

Sometimes such dilemmas are not brought to the fore, like the one above, where the researchers had to make a decision. Instead, the actors negotiate quietly, among themselves, without reaching a definite conclusion. I believe that this course of action in small ways is common in everyday life. However, lacking such data, a good, clear illustration was provided during an interview with two women in a women's shelter. I brought up the dilemma by asking about it – it had not been out in the open before. The shelters had from the start made promises and considered the possibilites of keeping the help-seeking women's anonymity as their *raison d'être*. They contrasted their own protection of the women's identity to the authorities' way of handling the women. They emphasized this feature of the shelters in media interviews and on the posters that were put up in public places. There were, however, examples of how they saw it necessary to break these vows of silence. In one case, when a woman with a child had a mental breakdown, they called the social welfare office; the child was taken into custody and the woman sent to a mental hospital. In another case they called the police when two women had stolen things from the shelter.

At other times nothing was done. The very long quote below concerns such a case; but when talking about it, the women illustrate the reasoning of good and evil – how strict the promise of silence is taken, how other values may supersede it, and whether a betrayal is committed by keeping to the rule of anonymity or not. In this interview two women are present, called A and B, the interviewer is called I.

I: Are there any problems when they [the authorities] want to find out about things?
A: They *want* to find out too much. We try to keep our mouths shut. For example, the other day, we had a woman from another town, they tried to poke around in it. Then there was a woman from the city who had just an awful background and at her request I contacted her social worker. She asked the whole time, "Where is she? What's your relation to her? Where's she living?" And I gave an off-the-wall answer and said that there was no reason for me to tell her. Here's her telephone number instead. . . . And of course you can always worm the secret number out of someone, we've been told. And we've said that

regarding the authorities, you are anonymous. We don't disclose your names if you don't want us to and give us permission.

I: Is that one of the holy rules?

A: Yes, for me it is.

I: Does it ever happen that you have to say "Stop! That's it?"

A: Yeah, in these incest cases. Then you are guilty of official misconduct if you keep your mouth shut. . . . But we are guilty of official midconduct [said quietly with a slight tone of shame in her voice]. One day this young mother with two children comes blowing in through the door and the little child had been sexually abused incestuously and she begged and pleaded with us not to say anything.

B: But she was going to do something about it, she was on her way out of the relationship.

A: I wonder. . . .

I: Classical moral conflict?

A: In those cases you should turn them in if they don't do something about their situation.

B: Yeah, in those cases they should be turned in.

A: Yeah – you have to think of the child there. A little three-year-old girl. She was so badly hurt.

B: Children should never have to suffer from the actions of adults.

A: You know the mother had been aware of it. Britt here got all white in the face.

B: Yes, I walked out. I can't handle it.

A: Same here, but I've seen it before at the day-care center. There it is a clear-cut duty to report such things – otherwise it is an instance of official misconduct. So I was really caught in a trap and looked at this little, injured child. And she [the mother] knew it! Once this man had had intercourse with her [the mother] while the children were watching. To be sure, under a couple of blankets, but. . . . My skin crawled – I just wanted to hit her! Such primitive feelings you get! I really had to get a hold of myself. . . .

I: Is that were you draw the line, that she goes?

A: Ahhh, we should have reported it in any case. Plainly and simply, we acted wrongly. But it's hard – you have a person in front of you crying and pleading and saying that she'll get in touch with a child psychologist.

I: The obligation to report, OK, but is it a formal one?

A: In my real job [pre-school teacher], yes, it's in the law.

I: But I mean here.

A: Yes, I think so.

A: Mmm. But formally?

B: Yeah, but if you find out that a crime is going to be committed and don't report it, then you're an accessory.

A: She said she was going to a child psychologist. But they also have an obligation to report it, you see! I told her that. Because I thought that I had to tell her, so that she knew. After that, we haven't heard anything. She called a few weeks later and told us that she got a place to live in another town. But since then she hasn't gotten into contact with the other woman who lives here, an allright woman that we are in contact with. So I wonder. . . . I think about the child. . . .

B: One ought to find out where she is.

A: I have her sister's telephone number and some other stuff – for the child's sake.

B: Of course for the child's sake. I think we should. If she doesn't take her, she gets reported. That's the only right thing. Let's do it!

I: But you say that you guarantee anonymity, it says so on your paper?

A: Mmm. In regard to the authorities, yes. But that was the woman. I don't know – what do you do? We could use some guidance here.

I: There is child abuse and. . . .

B: Yeah, it's the same thing. . . . It's possible that when we rewrite the rules, we'll say that when a child is involved. . . . For they can't expect everything from us. They can't expect that we will protect them when it's a question of criminal activity. . . .

I: It must be hard to decide sometimes. . . . The woman must consider it like a punishment if the child is taken into protective care, for example.

A: Yes, but often the thing is sparked off by the father doing something to the children, then he's gone too far. Then they leave. And in that case no one would be doing her a favor in taking the children away from her when she's finally gotten her act together and left. And then report to the authorities that the child has been beaten. To me it's taking away all her desire to fight.

A: No, it has to be an acute case. Let's say that she left and is living with us, goes out for a walk, and the husband attacks the child. Then. . .

B: Or you know that it is someone who has had contact with us and one assumes that child abuse has occurred, but that she has gone back to him again. But really, it has happened to me *once* that I knew about but in that instance, the social authorities were already involved.

I have included this long quote since I believe that it illustrates the many areas of uncertainties of a principle when meeting real-life experiences. As all principles, the holy rule of silence is one where one quickly finds exceptions.[26] The shelter women saw a situation where they had to choose between the woman's and the child's welfare[27] – a question of whom one betrays when keeping one's promises. One way of solving it was, as shown in the interview, to state that she was promised anonymity, not the child. (This seems rather far-fetched logic, however, if the shelters implement it as policy. If this becomes part of the program, it may cause women who are also mothers to hesitate before going to them.) Furthermore, a new norm seemed to have emerged: letting one keep one's promises of silence and anonymity, if the woman is "doing something about her situation." If the women keep in touch, perhaps seek help from a psychologist, etc., this may be interpreted as "good behavior."[28] Then, however, the question arose whether one should inform the woman that if she seeks the professional help in the form of a psychologist as they advise, the professional will be obliged to report the child to the social authorities. And how should this obligation to make an official report be interpreted in general? When does it apply? In the beginning of the interview one of the women tended to transfer her previous working experience to the shelter.   At her former workplace it was her duty to report.   Later in the interview though, she did differentiate the two situations. But then, they ask themselves: how about the duty to report that concerns all citizens – they are, after all, ordinary citizens even when working in the shelter. . .? It is also very clear that the issue is not clear-cut but is instead very uncertain; there are very few instances of black-and-white issues. Furthermore, the issue is "fixed" to such a small degree that during a short period like this interview, one may change or redefine one's position. The women clearly got more and more heated up during the talk and started acting almost as if they were prosecutors instead of the woman's defenders. After I left, I wondered for a long time whether they actually did report the woman . . . and whether I had acted as a catalyst for a betrayal.

Notes

1. Obviously we are also required to inform in some instances as discussed elsewhere in this book. Most states, however, recognize the limits of competeting loyalties so that there are certain exceptions to one's duty as a witness – relatives as an example. The lack of these rights among some societies is probably the one people find the most repellent. Literary illustrations, such as the frightening picture of the future in *1984*, use this theme; and one of the atrocity stories about German life during the Nazi era was about the Hitler youth and children who were being encouraged to report on their closest relations.

2. The fact that teaching small children not to tattle is not a

straightforward, easy task, depends perhaps on our teaching them other values first. These values may also be more concrete, such as the "no-no" things. These can then be coupled together under a general concept such as mischief. If one wants to teach them not to inform, one has to teach the value of "loyalty," which is abstract and may be more difficult to make concrete. In addition, children are often very keen on keeping and enforcing the rules once they have learned them. Learning not to tell about something one has just learned to be wrong is obviously no easy task. For example: I once read the Lucky Luke story, "Angivaren" (Chasseur de Primes), to Karl, a four-year old boy. In it there is a nasty bounty hunter who started his career as a "tattler." "Why did he do wrong?" the child asked me. I tried to explain the moral by exemplifying with a situation where his best friend, John, did a "no-no" thing and Karl then went to his friend's mother and told her. "This is tattling and it is not nice," I said. He nodded agreement and said: "No, it would not be nice if John did a no-no thing."

3.   "He" would perhaps not be equally damaged by telling. This would depend on whom he tells and in what cultural contexts. For other complications in the potential extortion situation of extramarital affairs, see Richardson (1988).

4.   In Haugen (1983) another problem is also discussed – the strategies of how to avoid becoming known as a gossip while still meeting the social demands and requirements of being informed.

5.   I will refer to "silence" here, as one mostly does, in speech or written documents. But in reality, this is not enough, since it is possible to tell through one's facial expression, body language, and so on. It is said of one who lets his emotions show that "his face gave him away," or that "one can read him like a book." When one succeeds in concealing one's thoughts, one is said to have a "poker face." Goffman has discussed possibilities of betraying or communicating the non-intended in such expressions under the heading "dramaturgic discipline." (1959, 217)

6.   It should be stated perhaps, that obligations and rights for different civil servants and professions, criminals, etc. are differently applied in different countries. I limit myself to general patterns of Western democratic societies.

7.   When formal rules or laws are made to ensure avoidance of betrayal, exceptions are often made. In principle, doctors maintain professional secrecy but must make a report if they suspect child abuse. Sometimes such rules are not general but might apply to those working in the public sector. In a book by Nonet and Selznick, they compare the situation for those seeking care for venereal diseases from public institutions with that for those who go to a private practitioner. The former group risks having it known that they suffer from such a disease because the staff at public institutions must try to elicit as much intimate information as possible so that their partners can be treated: ". . . all those named and identified by the unfortunate

lover, must be reached by the investigators. The women are called up at their homes or jobs, visited or written to, and finally (through motivation or fright) brought into the clinic. . . . One can imagine what family conflicts and even tragedies are created by this interference with the private lives and the bedrooms of people. Notice that those who can afford to consult a private physician escape all the official reports and investigations and are never asked for their contacts." (Nonet and Selznick 1978, 38–39) I imagine that those who believe all doctors maintain professional secrecy as their code of ethics must experience this as a betrayal.

8. Softley (1980) has shown quantitatively that older criminals as well as those with a previous criminal record choose to keep silent more often than others who are interrogated.

9. Peterson (1984) has described how even the legality of the promise for anonymity in a contract between a governmental agency giving the grant and the researchers was questioned when the fund givers suddenly wanted the sources to be revealed.

10. It is interesting to note that silence can be interpreted as suspicious in its own right (i.e., even if it does not follow after a specific question). If a group falls silent when one enters, one tends to believe they are hiding something from one, gossiping about one, etc., even though in reality it might simply be a question of gathering oneself as a group before the new member – adjusting. In other words, silence is easily interpreted as suspicious even if the group just falls silent in order to "regroup" to include the newcomer or if its members simply run out of topics.

11. Clamming up may also acquire a value of its own and become a norm in some groups, such as prison inmates. Those employing this technique come close to being glorified by inmates whether the technique was instrumental or not.

12. The high psychological costs in general of living with lies are illustrated by Montanino (1984) in a study of federal witnesses who were given new identities.

13. Excusing oneself with "I did not know" has its limits for superiors. In some serious cases this is no viable line of defence since they are supposed to know, and to take the responsibility even if they do not.

14. Another way of guarding one's sources when pressured to reveal them is to make them difficult to check. This seems to be a variation close to anonymizing. In *Russian Purge* the authors describe how the interrogation during 1936-1939 always contained questions about who recruited them and who they had recruited themselves for counter-revolutionary work. The ingenious way of avoiding betrayal was to name people who were dead or had left the Soviet Union forever: "An Armenian priest we came across had an excellent memory and was able to confess to having 'recruited' every single Armenian he had buried during the past three years. Frequently the cell into which one was put had a list available of dead people whose names could be drawn on for the purpose. The occupants of the cell changed rapidly,

and the list of names was passed from mouth to mouth; knowledge of it saved many." (Beck and Godin 1951, 57)

15. For a discussion on this particular ethical problem, see Junker (1960, 135–137).

16. This is one of many instances where relations between lies and betrayal are interesting. As with the morality of lies, in other contexts, such as in police work, it is coupled with a weighing of avoidance of harm. Other justifications that figure in police work (Klockars 1984b) are the lie as a technique for reaching the truth, and cutting red tape.

17. As shown in chapter 6, B), inmates believe they can identify informers by watching who gets rewarded. Such sign searching may, however, be wellknown as this prison officer's statement shows and therefore it can be counteracted. Betrayal of this sort seems to easily acquire a game-like quality and to the parties a satisfaction in itself. The prison officer here seemed quite pleased with himself.

18. Avoiding "bad newcomers" beforehand could also be done through insisting on a long apprenticeship like among printers or making it necessary for older members "to speak" for a new entrant, like among miners.

19. Goffman, labeling this strategy "vital test," reports however a Dear Abby letter advising a suspicious wife in this line. (1986, 98–99)

20. Other reasons obviously are to keep the group pure and to prevent its members from realizing that other alternatives are available.

21. One may, of course, use such rules, as always, for other ends. A part of a campaign to block the Swedish Electrolux Company from buying the American company Murrays was to sue Electrolux for insider information. The suit concerned whether Electrolux had been given secret information since both companies used the same law firm. (*Sydsvenska Dagbladet*/Swedish Daily/May 14, 1988, p. 21) Another aspect of this is how attorneys may beat this rule by getting one of the parties' consent. The party may, however, not understand what he agrees to. This "counter-strategy" is discussed in Mann (1985).

22. *Lagen om anställningsskydd* (LAS), chapter 6, Article 1.

23. In relation to this, Coser makes some interesting comments on sexuality as a potential competing force. Some greedy organizations thus advocate celibacy, such as Jesuits and the early Leninists. Others, such as the American Utopian societies, advocated "free love." Coser shows how celibacy and promiscuity may fulfill identical sociological functions.

24. Goffman (1959, 91, 212) discusses such unreliables in connection to the possible destruction, though not necessarily betrayal, of performances.

25. In one case the empathy is transferred to someone close to a resident who did inform. Wieder relates one incident where a mother called a parole agent about her son and he told her that he was sick. In commenting on the call he says: "I told her her son was sick. How

could I tell her that her son was in a special section for his own protection because he had snitched?" (Wieder 1974, 163)

26. It is possible that the Catholic church is the only institution honoring silence "no matter what" today.

27. If one chooses the child, another matter comes up – something that these women did not discuss, but others have. Even if a child has a bad situation, it might get worse if the social authorites take over.

28. In an American study (Ferraro 1983) from a women's shelter, it is reported that some women were thrown out – at times in a situation where they risked their lives – if they did not agree to the recommended proceedings, which often involved psychological counseling.

6

A One-Context Analysis: Crime and Informers

Three different issues will be addressed below concerning the specific type of betrayers who are called informers, and more precisely those who are so-called by their criminal associates.

Two of the areas concern the prison population's view of the informer, more commonly known as the snitch. First, two prominent "beast groups" in prison will be compared: sex offenders and the informers. Second, the process and search, and final decision concerning the identity of the informer will be discussed. Third, the snitches themselves will be analyzed.

Although these analyses are written with one group and one context in mind, many parallels can be drawn from other contexts. They were written before I started to think about the problem as a possible book and thereby had a freer hand. The first part of this issue explores the differences in the contempt toward sex offenders and informers in prison. While the first group was certainly harassed, the latter group was more treated with more contempt, never to be forgiven and a subject of much speculation. Although I have not found another context where two "beasts" as social types are so neatly presented as in prison, the obsession-like quality in talking, speculating about, and finding the informer can also be seen in such a diverse context as the school (Willis 1977), and in the Resistance. As to the latter, Aubert (1965) noted that people were more worried about possible informers than about the enemy during World War II in the Norwegian Resistance.

As to the second issue discussed, how the betrayer was found in a context where information was limited, the illustrations are numerous. In every situation where one knows someone must be responsible for leaking vital information but does not know *who*, one must conduct a search and make decisions on the identity of the culprit. When betrayal is done in the dark it opens up the market for group sharing and consolidation of pieces of information. Even in contexts where much of the informing is done openly, the remaining shadows might still be a matter of speculation. According to Navasky (1982), in spite of the great amount of research and debate about the "Hollywood informers" during the McCarthy era, no one yet knows how many did inform. In his book one can also find many self-saving explanations revolving around the stigma of being known as a betrayer, similar to those used by the criminal snitches I interviewed as analyzed in the third part of this chapter.

The analyses presented below originated from a study of violence and threats in Swedish prisons for which the material and method are described in the Appendix. They have been only slightly edited since they appeared as articles in *Deviant Behavior* ("Outcasts in Prison"), 7:1–12, 1986; *Deviant Behavior* ("The Social Construction of Snitches"), 9:155–167, 1988; and *Society* ("Snitches on Snitching"), 26, no. 2:22–26, 1989.

Outcasts in Prison
The Cases of Informers and Sex Offenders

Comment on snitches:

"It's a criminal society and the one who snitches can hardly expect to be accepted. When they did something they did it perhaps together. The guy who joins the other side, he's a traitor, no doubt about it."

Comment on rapists:

"They're often not the same type as the rest of us. They're a different kind of people, they're regular guys. . . . There's no place for them here."
"I don't know that they'd put in a request to come here (laughter)."
"Nah, but in any case, they should be allowed to go somewhere else. They don't have anything in common with us. It's the same with murderers. . . . There aren't any social reasons. You never know what to expect from them."

The literature on prisoners is extensive. Little attention, however, has been paid to the "outcasts among outcasts," that is, those stigmatized in prisons. Two such groups – the informers and the sex offenders – will be discussed here; or, rather, the different underlying reasons for the rejection they face from the other inmates. The two quotes above are ideal-typical illustrations of how the inmate society view their different outcasts.

The Two Groups

Those who are referred to as "snitches" here are those who have informed on other criminals or inmates either outside or in prison.[1] Most had informed outside prison and were subsequently harassed due to this factor. The sexual offenders in this study are those who have raped or sexually assaulted women or children outside prison.[2] Using Klapp's (1971) terminology, both social types represent "villains": the snitch, corresponding to "the traitor" and the sex offender as "the beast." Harassment or ill-feeling toward the two groups looks the same superficially. Members of both categories may be beaten up or forced to isolate themselves. There is, however, a qualitative difference in the moral condemnation of the two. The differentiating features of this condemnation can be presented schematically as a typology.

	Sex Offenders	Informers
Treatment and view of the villain		
1. Victim Status	Allowable	Obligatory
2. Attributed Responsibility	Questionable	Full
3. Attributed Motives	Irrational	Rational
4. Acceptance of Excuses	Can be Considered	No
Aim of Harassment	Sealing of status boundary	Sealing of norm boundary
		Deterrent
		Revenge

It should perhaps be added that it is the prescribed behavior and attitude or ideational moral that is analyzed below, not the actual treatment of the two outcast groups. Even if one states that excuses should never be accepted for informing, real life may provide situations where these are accepted anyhow.

Treatment and View of the Villain

Victim Status

First, there is a difference in victim status. Snitches are obligatory victims while sex offenders are allowed victims. A righteous inmate on snitches:

> "Does it happen sometimes that people get it for snitching?"
> "Yeah, when it's in front of you, in black and white."
> "Have you ever beaten up anyone?"
> "Yeah."
> "They should be punished like that?"
> "Yeah, they *have to*."

When inmates talk about sex offenders they take another view. It is not considered necessary to harass them. They are also granted a certain leeway – if they are nice, if they have acceptable explanations for their behavior, they might even be tolerated. I think the following quote might be illuminating:

> "At Stångby [a local, small prison], there was someone who was up for child molesting. He seemed like a pretty good guy. Drank a hell of a lot – everything possible – having lotion and stuff."
> "He didn't have any trouble there?"
> "He didn't, but another guy came, one of those snitches, and I heard that he really got it."

As I see it, there are two reasons for the different treatments. First, there are instrumental reasons for a strong norm of harassment against snitches. Even though snitching is not an unusual phenomenon, it would be even more common if the group did not make its members believe in reprisals. An English researcher, who has studied a prison designed to accommodate both informers and those sentenced for sex-related crimes, makes this point. He says that sex offenders are treated a bit more leniently by the other prisoners, and that: "Betrayal merits a more vindictive response because it endangers the livelihood and liberty of others who are engaged in illicit enterprises. The "grass," therefore, can go quite literally in fear of his life. (Priestly 1980, 35)

I believe that there is also another, perhaps more important, reason for the differences in attitude. Since sex offenders are viewed more distantly

– as an out-group – they do not have to be harassed. Conflicts, as we know from Simmel's analysis, are always more intensely felt when they occur in more intimate or in-group contexts.

During the interviews there was much talk of how the feeling concerning pursuing snitches had eased off from the good old days when they were supposedly always punished. There was also a lot of talk about good prisons, that is, those that harbored the tough clientele who would never accept a snitch among them. These prisons were the larger, more secure ones.[3] My interviewees complained about the lack of reprisals at the smaller, open prisons (where prisoners stay at the end of their sentences and which also house those committed for drunk driving and other inmates with short sentences). The complaint concerned "the lack of solidarity," i.e., pursuing snitches is seen as a manifestation of the common bonds of the prisoners or of the prison community in itself.

"Does it often happen that a snitch who moves to another prison is followed by his past? That people write letters and such."

"Yeah. That's the way it should be. It's too bad it isn't like that at all the prisons, but that's how it should be. It should end with him locked up in the mental wards. Unfortunately, that's not quite how it is at the small prisons. I've tried now with that Lena. I've tried to call Osterport [a small prison] to get the message through, but nothing's happened." [Lena was initially a prisoner at the interviewee's prison and was also a snitch.]

Sex offenders are, of course, also harassed; but their status as victims is allowable. This means that they are acceptable as victims if, for example, someone wants action or money. Their "beastly" crimes even legitimatize behavior otherwise condemned. Robbing other inmates is prohibited in the group for solidarity reasons, but it is not so unusual or taboo to rob groups in prison who are defined as "less than human." Sex offenders and gypsies are groups that, as we were told, have been robbed in prison. (This applies, of course, to those sex offenders who do not pass as "okay.") One inmate even used the attitude of the police to legitimatize his behavior:

"It was like this, see – there was this Italian who came here – he's been in 5 or 6 times for rape. He came from Karsudden [a mental institution] and was declared sane, even though they gave him a complete mental examination. So what happens – he raped a young boy. He claims now I beat him up and stole his money. That's why I'm here [at a ward for those who have broken regulations]."

"That's why you came here?"
"Yeah. First the cops questioned me – and you can see how they feel, too. The cop who questioned me, he started his questions by saying, "Don't worry – I'm not gonna put a lotta time on this. . . ."

Attributed Responsibility

Secondly, there is a difference in attributed responsibility. For other members of the criminal group, one demands full responsibility, but for sex offenders this is not quite the case. They are given "the benefit of the doubt," i.e., other inmates at times accept stories from rapers about women framing them. There are even responsibility-diminishing rationales at work when the crime is admitted. One such explanation is drunkenness, where the "real" self of the rapist or molester is not involved – he was "under the influence."[4] The most common explanation, however, is medical – as opposed to ordinary criminals, the sex offender is psychologically ill:

"Sure, they take small children and so on, nobody likes that. . . . But if you say that no normal person commits crimes, that's bull, 'cause anyone. . . . I mean, if you act like an animal, then there's something wrong upstairs. It's often like that. So it's wrong to put them in jail."

The most commonly recommended measure is incarcerating them in mental institutions, but castration is also suggested. What the inmates always point out, though, is that these people do no belong with Us, in Our prisons (which are for healthy, responsible people).

The nonresponsibility medical model is carried one step further: the interviewees tend to blame prison officials for the sex offenders' repeated crimes rather than the offenders themselves. They often state that it is wrong to let sex offenders out on leave or let them out of prison too soon because they cannot "help themselves." This view of them as not fully responsible can even mean that you feel pity for them as victims in prison:

"How the hell can they declare such a ding-dong sane? Beat little kids to death and then sexually abuse them. It's unbelievable. One time he's mentally ill, the next time he does it, he's sane! And they know how guys like that are treated in jail. You almost feel sorry for the guy, 'cause he's gonna have 10 years of hell."

This occasional sympathy is, however, not granted to the snitches. They are not to be sympathized with since they are seen as fully responsible for their crimes. An ideal typical view:

"I don't think they should be protected in the isolation wards."
"But what if they get beaten up?"
"They'll just have to take it!"

Attributed Motives

The third differentiating element that I have discussed is the attributed motives. Since sex offenders are often thought of as not being fully responsible due to reasons such as drunkenness or mental disturbances, their motives are also seen as irrational in the sense of not being fully comprehensible. They are often portrayed as "being swept away by sudden bursts of lust," for example. Many inmates are also morally indignant because the authorities give early releases to rapists or child molestors, because "sure enough, it happens again." The following quote illustrates the attitude quite well:

"The rapist, you know . . . there were three of them he raped on the train. He got three years. The week after he got here, he's sent on a trustee job outside the walls. You can really wonder where he's at, the prison director. After all, there's a school right next to us. And you never know when he's gonna get turned on."

Informers' motives, on the other hand, are seen as rational. Snitches are said to snitch because of greed or to get off more easily.[5]

Acceptance of Excuses

The fourth element that differentiates the groups in the view and treatment of other prisoners is in the acceptance of excuses.

Sex offenders may be excused. This is the case when they have raped someone older than approximately fifteen. Priestly (1980) even states that when someone is over fifteen years old, it is usually not even considered rape among English inmates. This is so because of the common "knowledge" that women tend to frame men or change their minds after the sexual act and scream "rape." Here then, we have initially a tough norm concerning sex offenders in general – perpetrators of unusual and bestial crimes – and then a "de-escalation" when you begin to discuss whom that norm applies to. As we have seen earlier, sex offenders may also be excused as being drunk at the time of the offence or simply being defined as "crazy."

The reverse seems to be the case when it comes to snitches. Even if a strong norm exists against snitching, a "normalization" of the crime is quite common. This is done through claiming that most criminals have snitched at some point during their career. From this, however, there seems to be an "escalation" of whom the definition is actually applied to, in the sense that behavior such as simply talking to guards may be labeled as snitching. Also, no excuses in principle are accepted. There have been cases when, for an outsider (us as interviewer, for example), a tolerance of the crime of snitching would be justified. This occurs when the talking has been done by someone close to the snitch – not by the snitch himself. An example of this are the instances when the police are said to have brought in somone's wife and threatened to implicate her as an accessory, even if she is innocent of the crime. This is a "snitch's" account:

"And when my wife was dragged off to the pits [held for questioning], I can hardly sit here and expect she'll keep her mouth closed, deny everything, and know about all the damned peculiar ideas they have here. She's like she is, she's a person, and completely naturally . . . if she can't hold on, I can certainly understand that. But to get that through some people's thick skulls. Then you shouldn't drag in those people, they say. I haven't done it either, but I'm married to her, and there's been people at home."

But this is never accepted as an excuse. The counter norm in the criminal group is "do not involve those that do not know the rules of the game." That one should not involve one's wife is an often repeated statement.

There are also other types of explanations that one, as an outsider, could think of as being examples of justifications. One is that someone is too young to have the experience to resist the police. This, however, is not accepted either as a valid excuse:

"Can you understand why someone would snitch on a chum?"
"No – I've never done it."
"But the police threaten and promise. . . ."
"Yes, but you can't believe them. They can't promise anything."
"What if you don't know that? If you're new?"
"You find out beforehand. You know. Some think it's hard to be arrested, and it is. But you got yourself into the situation."

We also asked about addicts' snitching since they are seen as the most untrustworthy. As Coleman (1975) has pointed out, addiction is seen as a justification for behavior that would not otherwise be accepted. This is so because the addiction in itself, the physical craving, is interpreted as being irresistible. Also, addicts are considered as being transformed into other types of people: unpredictable and untrustworthy. This then could correspond to the view of sex offenders being mentally disturbed or committing their crimes under the influence of alcohol (and hence transformed into other types of selves). The righteous inmates, however, did not think addiction was an acceptable excuse. In relation to informing, it was denied that drugs had as much effect as is said. A righteous inmate: "They just use abstinence when arrested to be able to say: I couldn't help but admitting, I couldn't take the pain.   That's rubbish. I've used drugs myself and they're never influenced me to the point where I lose control."

Aim of Harassment

The aim of harassment also differs between the two groups.   As has already been mentioned, deterrence is something that applies to snitches. This can be viewed theoretically as either a general deterrent by using someone as an example to prevent others from informing, or as an individual deterrent to prevent someone from snitching again. In reality the emphasis seems to be put on the general deterrent. The reason behind this, as I see it, can be attributed to the norm (even if not always followed) that if someone snitches, he will not be accepted in the criminal group again.

"Who is it who "takes care" of snitches?"
"Those who want to stay in the field. They want to get some kind of security for themselves, I think. They want to show others that if you mess up, it'll be hell on wheels in jail. People see that guys get beat up 'cause they mess up when they're in jail. If you go out and steal together after you've been behind the same bars, so to say, then when you're caught, you know that you can't say anything because the other guy will fix you good, or someone else will."

The revenge motive is, of course, also important when snitches are concerned – something not applicable to the sex offenders. The revenge, however, seldom seems to take the form of a direct confrontation betweem the snitch and the "snitched-on." If pure revenge is involved, the punishment is carried out mostly through intermediaries.   This is explained by two factors by the inmates. First, the one immediately involved would be suspected by the prison staff. Second, when court cases involve several people, they are often placed at different prisons, especially if one of them has informed on others.

There is, however, also another – more sociologically interesting – aim or purpose in punishing snitches (even if not consciously acted upon by individual group members), and this is in enacting group norms. The punishment can therefore be seen as serving both as a norm-maintenance device and as a *sealing of norm boundary*. The following quote illustrates this type of harassment that is not (directly, at least) instrumental:

"You said that your life was threatened."

"Yeah. I've gotten letters up here [on the ward]."

"Who writes these letters? The guys you were sent up with?"

"Nah, not those guys, 'cause no matter how strange it sounds, they know. . . .They've gotten copies of the investigation and 've been there with the cops. They know too that they were caught regardless of what I said, so they're not mad at me. It's the laws or rules in our group. It's other guys who were involved maybe in other business with me, who weren't mixed up in this particular caper. People all over the place, on the outskirts, who decide, and who think that I ought to have shut my trap regardless of what proof they [the police] had. Who then write to you."

"Do they have any reason to fear that you would testify against them?"

"No."

"Is it the morals of this issue?"

"Yeah. It's the morals."

The aim of harassing sex offenders on the other hand, is a matter of *sealing the status boundary*. This is a We and Them distinction. When they are not excused and therefore tolerated, their crimes are seen as so bestial that the individuals who commit them are not understandable. Punishing Them is a way of proclaiming that they are another sort of people and a sort We do not accept. This attitude was seen in some instances, i.e., on semi-isolated wards that harbored snitches and others. A couple of times we were told that, "Even here, we don't accept such people." This way of talking about sex offenders as "such people" or "one of those" was used by all prisoners. As I see it, it is a manifestation of the almost nonhuman status attributed to them.

Discussion

It is a usual reflection among sociologists that common enemies tend to unite a group and to clarify its moral boundaries. In a Durkheim mode of analysis, sociologists such as Erikson (1966) and Klapp (1971), have pointed out the role of deviant in this fashion. Similarly, criminologists have emphasized the cohesion-producing role of outcasts in prison. Both types of outcasts discussed here, the snitches and the sex offenders, tend to serve and support group morals as evil objects or social types that the inmate group can unite against.

In order to fully understand the differences in which the two groups are treated and viewed, I think that another classic thread of analysis is useful: Simmel's on different forms of conflict. In "Der Streit" he showed the difference between in-group versus out-group conflict. He wrote, for example, about conflicts being more intense in in-groups. This was very obvious among the inmates. When we asked about violence, threats or conflicts in prisons between inmates, the spontaneous and elaborated answers were always about snitches.[6] We often had to ask inmates specifically about their views of rapists and child molesters. When they answered, they tended to be quite expressive in their dislike but quickly left the subject. This is an expression, I think, of the self-evident negative definition they have at the same time as the out-group status gives a distanced view. This distance admits allowable victims instead of obligatory ones, as well as a certain acceptance of excuses not granted to snitches as discussed above.

The intensity can also be explained by the fact that the snitching individuals are often old friends of their pursuers. For their old friends, they are seen as not only betraying the group but also "me," because the identity given to "you" in the group is to a great deal formed by whom you associate with. The intensity of feelings or level of excitement that the group produces must necessarily be high to force you to condemn and reject an old friend. Maybe this explains what seemed a more ritualized harassment of snitches as compared with sex offenders. Trials by your peers were said to be at work when judging snitches. This was never mentioned in connection with sex offenders. Also gang beatings were more frequent according to the interviewees when it came to punishing snitchers, but not sex offenders.[7]

One can view the importance of the group in another way as well. Snitching is a crime against the group; and therefore, there exists a strong social control of the rejection of snitches. The norm, however, does not have to be internalized or private.

That the punishment of informers is mainly a group phenomenon is seen in the interesting situation when those who are considered the most active in "fixing" snitches land in the ward next to those of the snitches. This happens in prisons which have "regulation 20 wards" (which are for those persons who have broken certain regulations) and "regulation 18 wards" (for those requesting voluntary isolation) in the same physical area:

"And then the hardest ones come there too – to Reg. 20 [punishment ward] if there is an evaluation of something. And then you meet them there suddenly and you can talk to them as easy as anything. All of a sudden it's no big thing any more."
"So the attackers and the victims get to meet?"
"No, not really, they're not supposed to. But the wards were together there so that you could go from one to another even it if wasn't officially open."
"And then you could talk together?"
"Yeah. Then it wasn't a big deal any more, because you were all in the same boat suddenly, so it didn't matter that you'd snitched."

Most inmates avidly preach group morals and have strong feelings about the rules against snitches and the punishments for snitching. At the same time, there are some who are just followers, who go along with freezing people out, or threaten them because it is the easiest way to fit in with the group – it costs too much not to. They say, for example, "I had no choice" or "that's just the way it is." Regardless of the individual's previous identity, the need to fit in can lead to a moral change depending on the context one finds oneself in.

"Are snitches safe there?" [in a therapeutic ward for drug addicts].
"Yeah, there's not one who can get at you there. If a person comes in, his morals are changed: 'I don't give a damn if it's a snitch, I'm going to get out of here. And stop doing drugs and such. So I don't give a damn if they're snitches – it doesn't affect me.' It's the group pressure that does it."

Finally, the group-bound nature of the harassment of informers is shown in the very definition of a snitch: a snitch is someone who is a member of the group (this is why the toughest punishment is defined as being rejected by the group, not by being beaten up). When he disclaims membership, he is no longer a snitch.[8]
One of the interviewees said that he had to give up crime because he had snitched. He said at first that he was threatened and therefore afraid

regarding his impending release.   However, he added the following reflections:

"But at the same time when you're released. . . You say that you've called it quits with the old life and you've stopped turning on. Somehow, the past is forgiven and forgotten [that you snitched] and people accept that you're out of it now and don't give a damn what you did before. You see?"
"Yes."
"That's how it works.   They don't make the same demands on that person."

Notes

1. The little that is available has mainly been content with declaring that the role of the "rat" or the snitch exists and is negatively valued. (Clemmer 1940; Schrag 1944; Bowker 1977, 1980;).   Other writers, such as Johnson (1961) and Wilmer (1965), have focused on types and personality attributes of "rats." Priestly (1980) has studied the prison situation for harassed inmates (among them informers).   Marquart and Roebuck (1985) have studied a rather special prison ward that guards and influential prisoners cooperated in running, with the latter group acting as snitches.   Finally, Ward and Kassebaum (1965) and Ward (1982) have studied the reasons why women prisoners inform.
2. Rape in Swedish prisons is something one never hears of, i.e., it is something that does not occur or occurs very seldom. Sexual relations in prisons are extremely rare, maybe because of relatively short sentences. (Bondeson 1974)
3. "Big" in Sweden means about threehundred and fifty prisoners instead of about fifty.
4. According to McCaghy (1968) this is quite a common explanation given by child molestors.
5. Plea bargaining is not legally accepted in Sweden, but inmates and prison officials claim that it exists informally. According to the same sources, informers can also be allowed to serve their sentences in "easy" prisons, i.e., relatively small and open.
6. Compare McCleery (1960) who writes about inmates being obsessed by the subject.
7. Sylvester et al (1980) have shown that multiple-assailant homocides in American prisons are more ritualized and occurs when the victim is suspected to be a snitch, involved in gang fighting or in drug business. Single-assailant homocides on the other hand are triggered by homosexuality, debts etc. Priestly (1980), however, mentions gang-beatings of sex offenders in England.
8. Maguire (1982, 78) points out that: "It is interesting that receivers who made statements to the police were said to be forgiven more easily

than thieves, perhaps because they are not seen as fully members of criminal groups." Others such as Klockars (1974) have emphasized the importance of fences for the economic system of criminal groups as a reason for them being leniently treated if they inform.

The Social Construction of Snitches

The information on who is a snitch is reputed to travel through the prison grapevine. Shibutani's (1966) work on rumors will be used for describing the social conditions necessary for rumors to flourish when they appear and for his emphasis on them being social constructions. Luhmann's (1979) work on trust will also be used. His basic argument is that we routinely act even though we have insufficient information.

While analyzing the interviews I found two concurrent but conflicting themes. On the one hand, most of the interviewees said that "almost everyone has snitched." By this they mainly referred to informing outside the prison. Snitching was also said to be more common today than in the "good old days" when thieves were more "honest" and when a smaller proportion of the criminal population was made up of addicts (who are believed to be more snitch-prone):[1] "The old honor among thieves has completely vanished. . . . The fact that they're on drugs means that they sing more to the police. You can't really feel secure in jail. You can't trust anyone."

On the other hand, there is a tendency to point to one in a prison as the snitch, or a few as the snitches. Furthermore, it is a common belief that a snitch will always be discovered and will get "what he deserves." As one inmate said: "It doesn't matter which jail you're in, there's contacts, the word always gets out. Even if it's not really serious. Even if ya' never got no one in serious trouble. All ya' gotta do is talk too much, that's it, that's the ball game."

The identity of the informer is thus both something obvious – everybody knows who he is – and at the same time a social construction[2] (since almost everybody has snitched at some time[3]).

"How do you know who snitched?"
"Yeah, that's also surprised me. I mean, how the hell we found out. Every time, it's crystal clear . . . a guy comes in from a holding cell or

somewhere else on the outside, and info about things gets built up. And of course ya' don't go out and nail a guy if ya' just have a feeling, nothing more. But . . . ya' *know*."

The Social Construction

Informers are harassed both in a psychological and physical way. Even if murders of inmates by other inmates are said never to happen in Swedish prisons (as compared to the United States where some of the victims are informers), they still run the risk of encountering violence. In other words, it is obviously in their best interest to hide their betrayals.

In cases other than when two or more partners in crime stand trial together and one knowingly and publicly informs, the snitch has to be identified through a search. The reason for doing this is a belief in upholding norms as ends in themselves, upholding norms to prevent potential informers, and a desire for revenge. Inmates also tend to believe that "once a snitch, always a snitch." Staying at the same ward as someone who has once informed outside prison makes life in such a ward insecure. The situation is thus characterized by some inmates trying to hide an identity while this is much searched for by others.

This serves as the backdrop for rumors about snitches being so common in prison. As Shibutani (1966) has noted for rumors, and Yngvesson (1978) and Bailey (1971) for gossip, such communication develops when people are caught in ambigous situations.

The main sources for discovering informers, according to the interviewees, are personal communication, signs such as otherwise unearned privileges, types of wards and prisons where sentences are served, talking to guards, motives, and court and/or police records. These will be addressed separately below.

First of all, inmates naturally *talk* to each other about people whom they believe to be informers. When someone arrives at a prison the residents are curious about this newcomer, and they discuss him along themselves. Sometimes someone has a reputation as a snitch before he comes to a new prison:

"There was one guy here who first asked to be isolated and then was transported to another prison. And then you heard that now he's there, now he's in Kumla, and now he's in Norrköping, every place he'd been at. . . (laughter) . . . Somebody always found out who he was, wherever he went."

Those who communicate this type of information do not need to be the ones identified by the snitch. They are often "interested parties" who wish to maintain the morals and who are upholding the norms of the criminal group; or they are simply interested in some "action."

Sometimes this type of information is judged to be enough. There is among these groups, as in others, a tendency to make an "overdraft on information," as Luhmann (1979) has written. Luhmann argues that since our society is too complex and includes too much information for one ever to be absolutely sure, it is necessary to make decisions based on practical information, both because time is a limited resource and because our psychological makeup demands conclusions. This is a simplifying strategy, used by all and in many social contexts. Even if "too much information" is not the problem in the prison situation, I believe the same strategy is occurring here.

The tendency of making an overdraft on information is especially strong if the carrier of information is someone respected among the inmates. Such persons will have a greater say in typifying people than the average inmate – a *greater definitional power* than others. Consequently, it is in their power, apart from successfully labeling someone, to also free inmates from being labeled: "I saved a guy, I did it, ya' know. . . I was sittin' in his cell when these guys [who were going to beat him] came in, see – and I says, Hey, hold on, damn it, this here guy is Grade A, he aint a snitch."

This interviewee constructed this information only from knowing the suspected inmate as "a good guy." The reason that the others went along with his judgment of the man was that he had proved himself to be trustworthy. This had been done through testifying falsely on a previous occasion in order to save these same attackers when they had beaten up another snitch. He had done this voluntarily – without them asking for it – a "supererogatory performance," as Luhmann (1979) names one basis for trust.

Guards, who are normally not considered reliable concerning inmate affairs, are in this context sometimes mentioned as sources. They, too, can actually be viewed as having a greater definitional power than the average inmate. Among the inmates who were not accused of being snitches, some mentioned that guards had given them information. They did not say this out loud; but when I asked how they had found out about someone, they nodded conspiratorally in the direction of the guards' room. The strength of this belief can be shown by a man who had gotten a tip about someone he had known as a friend for years. In spite of this friendship, he acted on the guard's information and tried to get the other inmate harassed by telephoning the prison where this person had been moved.   Inmates never questioned guards' information although I encountered one inmate in an isolation ward who swore he was innocent of the charge of having informed and that he had been framed by a guard.

Maybe this information is trusted to such a high degree because it comes from the out-group and might be given a bit reluctantly, in confidence. As one said: "It's not said straight out – they give you a hint, sort of." Furthermore, this information is given quite seldom, which helps to foster the feeling of exclusiveness. It is thus not interpreted as ordinary gossip or "rumor-mongering." Finally, as for those who inform in prison, guards are seen as "in the know."

Getting "undeserved" or unaccounted-for *privileges* from an out-group is, I am sure, one of the most general bases for suspecting a member of a group of treachery. In my study, getting a sentence considered to be too light or doing one's time at a prison viewed as better than others or getting the prison sentence transferred to a rehabilitation center were examples of privileges that were interpreted as signs of informing outside prison. Getting day passes or a better job than other inmates were seen as signs pointing toward informing in prison.[4] Such privileges, combined with being seen *talking to guards*, could add up to a decision of someone being named an informer: "After three months, he got a trustee job. We see how he talks with the guards also . . . he gets paid for everything he does."

In another case, however, we were told by one inmate (talked about by others as a "righteous thief") about a similar case where the accused had been innocent. The reason for him being labeled a snitch and forced to ask for isolation was envy from other the inmates due to this man's day passes which, according to our informant, were a result of behaving like a "nice guy" – chattering about weather and such things to the guards.

What is said below should not be interpreted as saying that it is impossible to talk to or chat with guards – simply that there is a norm restricting this communication and that, probably, the lower you are in rank, or the more suspicious others are of you, the stricter this norm is applied.

That there is such a general group norm governing communication between guards and inmates is evidenced by the fact that inmates are privately more positive in their attitudes toward guards than they believe others are. (Bondeson 1974) This can be interpreted as a group norm having a symbolic meaning of differentiating "Them" from "Us." Another interpretation, however, might be that it is an instrumental norm restricting the communication in order to prevent information from the inmate group slipping out.[5] One of the reasons why the women in Ward's (1982) study could inform without being punished by their own group was that there was no norm against communication between the groups.

Ward (1982, 253) states that: ". . . the fact that women went about the grounds unescorted and that casual conversations with passing staff were quite normal and unremarked on meant that it was very difficult to pinpint the culprit when secrets had been revealed."
Another "sign" is that of having been to the *wrong prison or ward*. Some prison are seen as such because they have the reputation of harboring informers. This includes those wards to which those who ask for voluntary isolation are sent.

"If there's someone who's snitched and can't protect himself, he get placed in that ward. And it's hated by the rest, there're all the bastards. But there's also a lot there who just can't take the cons and they get the same reputation."

This was said by one staying at such a protected ward, stating that he was there because he needed a retreat from ordinary prison life. His belief that most of the ordinary inmates were lumped together in this manner was shared by most in the protected wards. This, however, was not always the case. I heard several prestigious inmates talking about (with some condescension however) other inmates who cannot mentally handle ordinary prison life and who therefore, isolate themselves. These people were not believed to be informers.
The prisons that are considered as having a greater share than normal of snitches are judged this way for two reasons. First, some prisons are thought of as more safe than others so that some are sent there as a protection from other inmates. Second, one prison, Österåker, tries to rehabilitate addicts. This is done in part through therapy groups, where the inmates are expected to be as "open" as possible. In the view of other inmates, these inmates become – even if not starting out as such – snitches. An inmate at Österåker said: "Everybody knows that it's only bastards and snitches who are here. But it's not like that."
Coming from this particular therapy-oriented prison to a common prison was in some instances reported to have led to inmates being beaten up for this reason alone which is an interesting latent function of modern rehabilitation. Having done time in a tough prison can enhance one's reputation, while the rehabilitative ward or prison creates a stigma.
Motives of various kinds were seen as evidence of being a snitch by the accusers. This evidence, however, was mostly used in combination with other information sources. Examples of such mentioned motives were those of inmates who wanted to get rid of a competitor in drug dealing and therefore were giving tips to the police or the prison staff about the opponent's activity. Other examples are revenge for cheating in business

deals, or for stealing someone's girl friend or lover. An illustration of the latter is presented below.

"But you never gave testimony in court?"
"No . . . but if me and this girl hadn't said something [to the police], they would've gotten off. Instead, he got seven [years]. And . . . I'm also in on my girl's testimony. But they don't get that – he believes that this is my revenge since he moved in with her."

That he had informed and that his motive was revenge was, he said, spread through the grapevine so now "everybody knows that this is how it was." According to him, he was no informer since he had only confirmed some of the things his former girl friend had already told the police. This was also the picture we got through reading their police and court records. His situation, however, was made worse and his argument judged less reliable since he had stayed at the therapy-oriented prison referred to above.

Rumors built on personal communication and signs are not always granted a high status. Such rumors are often interpreted as untrustworthy. Most inmates state that "you can't trust all the rumors," or "the ones who mouth off the most [about informers] often have bad consciences themselves." As Shibutani (1966) has pointed out, oral communication is often viewed as more unreliable and both rumors and gossip are talked about in derogatory terms. This type of information is not always enough to brand someone a snitch. Therefore, when one has quite strong suspicions, another strategy is used in order to settle the issue of definitely labeling someone. When inmates suspect someone, there is a practice in which he or she is asked to show his or her *papers* (for example, court records and sometimes police reports).[6]

This is often used to verify or falsify other sources of information. These papers are seen by most inmates as the ultimate proof. It is there, in black and white. One inmate explained: "There's a lot of talk. But you can't be sure until you've seen the papers. . . There's a lot of intrigues and people asking me, for example, to hit this or that guy so they'll go down to the isolation ward. Because of that I never believe anything until I've seen the papers."

Some inmates were not so easily satisfied. They believed that not even these papers were to be trusted if one was looking for informers. This was because the police could choose not to write down (in transcripts) everything that was said during an investigation. This is known as a way of "paying" for information. (This practice, although forbidden in Swedish law, has been confirmed in some interviews I have had with the police.) In one interviewee's view: "It's a trade off, they get rid of a couple of things. Just put it away. Maybe there's two thefts – OK, we take those away if you tell us how it really is. . . . So in principle papers don't mean a thing."

This attitude according to what we heard later, did not prevent the same man from asking later on for papers from someone he suspected of being an informer. Thus one seems to believe and use the available pieces of information if they support a case – this can also mean supporting a belief in someone's innocence.

A final comment is in order about the practice of using papers. The papers had acquired a semisacred character; they were carefully kept and compared with trusted others. As one policeman said: "They are kept and read as if they were love letters." If they disappeared, one worried even when, as in one case, they made no difference when it was time to prove his innocence. When one talks to inmates or someone from the staff, they point out how suspicious the atmosphere has become in comparison to the "good old days"; and that these days "everybody" has to show his papers. That this is not so, however, is discovered when asking "righteous" inmates if they ever have shown their papers.

"Do you have your papers with you?"

"Yes – if someone comes in here and says something to me, that I snitched on so and so: 'Look at my papers!'" So far there's no one's ever done it, but. . . ."

"Protection?"

"Yeah – but if someone came in and said . . . then I don't know how I'd react. I'd probably bash him in the head."

Being asked to present one's papers is thus a sign of distrust and is seen as offensive.

The different sources of information are seen as more or less trustworthy. As I have tried to show, the inmates accept some information and reject other information in order to prove or refute that someone is an informer. This is also Shibutani's general view of how rumors are constructed: "The common definition that eventually arises takes shape through the adoption of some views, the elimination of others, and the gradual integration of those items that have *survived*." (1966, 178)

Even though in many (perhaps most) cases the branding of informers is done on reasonable grounds, in some cases the labeling is a result of "invalid sign-searching." This makes it possible to "steer" in this social construction. Hence, we can note – even if our material does not allow us to dwell on it – that we encountered several stories of how the police and the prison guards (sometimes out of revenge or malice) spread true or false information about someone being an informer.[7] We were also told about inmates who spread rumors about others they wanted to get rid of such as competitors in love or in business.

Consensus

Despite the uncertainty in knowing who is a snitch, when a conclusion is finally drawn inmates express a high degree of conviction. This might be explained by saying, as Shibutani (1966) notes, that overt acceptance of a rumor may become a symbol of loyalty to the group. Furthermore, he points out that when a group has finally drawn a conclusion, there is a demand on everybody to agree to this interpretation. If someone still disagrees, group sanctions will be applied: "Only a few are able to withstand such pressure, and even those who privately remain unconvinced acquiesce in their overt conduct." (Shibutani 1966, 144)

This state of affairs was very typical among the inmates. Several testified that unless one avoided informers, one would be in trouble. If one socializes with someone who is labeled a snitch, this is seen as going against the group – the common definition – and one's own motives will be questioned. Ultimately one will be treated as a snitch oneself. One inmate talked of how he had been unfairly labeled and had the sympathy of a few others, but they did not dare show this sympathy openly:

"The snitches are frozen out, there's no one who'll talk with them. People don't *dare*. Most everyone doesn't dare – the average John Doe, like me, ya' know – they just wanna do their time and be left in peace."

Social Context

Different pieces or sources of information have been discussed so far. However, I briefly want to touch upon the importance of the social context for the construction of "snitches." Labeling is, as Becker (1963) among others has pointed out, always dependent on the social context – on the audience and the situation and not only on the act.[8] Whether or not someone will be labeled depends on such things as whether moral entrepreneurs are available and the social characteristics of those harmed. Both these things were important according to the interviewees.

Furthermore, there was said to be less talk about and branding of informers at the local, smaller prisons where inmates were imprisoned toward the end of their sentences. This was so, they said, because if someone started a fight or did anything else that could be interpreted as misconduct, they would be moved to a central prison with tighter security – someting considered much less attractive. Studies have also shown prisoners to be less involved in the issue of solidarity when they are getting ready to leave. At such times prisoners contemplate socializing with other groups. (Glaser 1969; Åkerström 1985a)

Finally, as has been shown above, the social category "snitch" is not clear-cut. Maybe the most important element is that it is so strongly group related. For criminals, the "straights" as outsiders are never "snitches" but "witnesses" when they inform about a crime. To "snitch" you must inform on someone who has socially legitimate claims on you not to tell. This means that it is not enough to be a criminal or to be accused of a crime in order to expect to be protected by "the code." This account from a thief who had just been condemning informers is revealing:

"I *testified* against someone once, yeah, I did. And I did it without hesitating and of my own free will . . . there was this guy who beat up on a fourteen year old girl. He battered her whole face . . . in that case ya' can *testify* against someone with a clear conscience and not be scared. But otherwise it's best to keep your trap shut." (Emphasis added.)

In other words he is not defining himself as a "snitch."

Discussion

It has been shown that when the role of snitch is there, it has to be filled. The subject of informing is an important topic among criminals. This is evidenced in McCleery's (1960) claim that uncovering snitches is an obsession for the majority of inmates. Furthermore, Maguire (1982, 76) writes in a study of burglars, "We were surprised at the prominence the subject [informing] seemed to take in discussion among thieves. . . ."

This strong interest can be viewed as a sign of a *shared concern*. If it were interpreted as someone's individual concern and perhaps as a matter of private revenge, then this would not be a theme for common gossip. The social motives underlying this common concern are based on both moral norms and an instrumental interest. This concern can thus be seen as a sign of a collective attitude. As Shibutani has put it in his analysis of rumors, "Only when a multitude of persons are sufficiently aroused by the same possibility does a rumor develop. Unless sensitivities are shared, people will not even talk for long about the same thing." (1966, 198) In prison reliable information is often scarce. In this situation one interprets and evaluates the available knowledge of rumors and signs, and ends with the certainty which the interviewee reported in the beginning expressed as: "It's crystal clear!"

Notes

1. For this type of belief that most inmates in a prison are people who at some time have snitched on others outside prison, see Maguire (1982). For the belief that addicts are most snitch-prone, see most of the "crime as a career" literature or "crime as lifestyle." (Åkerström 1985a)
2. "Social construction" is not used here as a concept describing something that is more or less an artifact, but as a construction of different pieces of information building a social definition.
3. Softley (1980 80, 82) confirms in a study of police interrogation that many do tell on their associates.
4. The same tendency can be seen in the studies by Morris and Morris (1963), Navasky (1982), and Ward (1982).
5. This is comparable to statements by the police that when they meet their informers out in the streets they do so discreetly. This is not due, I believe, to criminals always having a grudge against the police. It is acceptable to talk to the police if you are in a group, but standing alone and talking to an officer is viewed more suspiciously.
6. Police records are given out when releasing them can no longer hinder an investigation.
7. See Pepper (1979) for a similar account of the police branding the author as an informer in revenge because he would not inform.
8. As for differentiating sanctionings of informers, see Ward and Kassebaum (1965), Giallombardo (1966), and Ward (1982) who claim a higher incidence of informing and lesser sanctions in prisons for women than in prisons for men. McCleery (1960) states that the labeling and prosecuting of informers depends on the level of ambiguity in prison units. Marquart and Roebuck (1985) describe a prison where during a specific time period the informers were actually those in power.

Snitches on Snitching

So far the reasons for informers being treated intensively with contempt and the inmates' identification of the informer have been discussed. Below the the focus is on the snitches themselves. How do they cope with being defined as such? How do they explain this generally denounced label to themselves and others?

Resisting the Label

The labeling approach is a much used and commonly known perspective in sociology, especially concerning labels considered negative. Stringent theoretical analyses of the countering and avoidance of such labels have been less common. Prus (1975) has outlined such a systematic analysis based on numerous substantive studies dealing with the management of deviant identities. He identifies five major forms of resistance tactics: challenging the designation, challenging the designating agent, resisting by relocation, resisting by reappealing, and resisting through compromise.

The three forms found among those I interviewed were challenging the designations, challenging the designating agent, and resistance by relocation. Several substrategies can be found within the forms. Some of those I discuss are mentioned by Prus; others are not. Many of them can be found in other analyses of how various stigmatized groups come to terms with their labels.

Two of the forms of resistance tactics that Prus mentions were not found in the interviews: reappealing and compromise. This might be due to sampling limitations, but I believe that this result mirrors a more general tendency. Resisting by reappealing (the repentant sinner) does not seem to be possible in principle since the system of norms of the other inmates states that a traitor is not to be forgiven, and his excuses are not to be accepted. Neither is the form of resistance by compromise feasible

119

since this is based on the victims having a bargaining power by possessing exchange potentials. According to Prus, a compromise of this kind can be achieved by jeopardizing the integrity of the accuser, for example, by using undesired name calling ("prejudiced" and "fascist"). This strategy seems impossible because the accusers are not comprised of one small group or a few individuals inside the collective but by the entire collective.

Challenging the Designation

One form of resisting a label is by questioning its appropriateness. This can be done through bringing up categorical inconsistencies as when mobsters try to counteract their villain image by making references to their charity donations, thereby acting contrary to their undesired characterization. (Klapp 1964) Another example is Cressey's (1953) account of embezzlers claiming not to be "thieves" but honest citizens who intend to repay their "loans."

The use of euphemisms by the interviewed was perhaps the most basic strategy of defense. None of those who had informed called it "informing" or themselves "informers." "Snitch" or "snitching" were absolutely taboo words.[1] In the beginning of the project a few informers probably slipped by unnoticed because the questions were not phrased with the right euphemisms. Since the area is so sensitive, I am convinced that some (whom others had identified as informers), held back and said they were staying at a protected ward for reasons other than having been branded as snitches (for example, that they failed to pay their debts to other inmates).[2] Because one of the research assistants was a former inmate, he was aware of the realities of prison life and came up with a solution to this problem. He suggested that we should start interviews by saying: "They have written so much in the newspapers lately about victims of violence and threats in prisons,"[3] – demonstrating sympathy. We should then continue: "A lot of inmates have been witnesses in courts – that's why, I guess," thereby normalizing the informing. Then we could pose a question something like: "Have you yourself said anything in court that. . . ?" This worked. I believe that even at this point it would have been too direct a question to ask if they "had given testimony." When those interviewed described the reason for their being placed in isolation, they said, for example:

"There was trouble."
"What kind of trouble?"
"Just some shit. Dealing with my trial. I confessed to something and another didn't own up to it."

Most used this type of evasive language. A few used more obvious euphemisms such as "taking responsibility for one's former activities," "to get rid of it," or "take a stand." These were inmates who had converted either to rehabilitation therapy, which advocated openness (the telling about one's former activities and sometimes also showing one's new loyalties by testifying in court[4]), or to religion. One inmate, for example, had gotten involved with Scientology.

As Prus (1975), and others (e.g., Sykes and Matza 1957; Taylor 1976; Navasky 1982) have noted, another common form of resisting designations is through disavowing responsibility. This is a more elaborate form of defense than the one discussed above. Here an explicit account is given. One acknowledges that the label is accurate "but I was forced to, because . . ." – special circumstances are given implying that one is not "really" a snitch.

Although plea bargaining is not allowed in Sweden, it is said that the police and the prosecutor promise shorter sentences in exchange for information. Some of the interviewees had been arrested for drug offenses committed earlier in their lives but had later stopped using narcotics and now had a job and a family. They saw cooperation as their only chance to save their new lives. Arguments such as "I had to" or "I couldn't do anything else" were also used by those who saw the police pressuring someone close to them. This could be done due to a law that states it is illegal to know about drugs being sold without reporting it. Thus it was claimed that many of the drug dealers' wives or girlfriends were threatened by the police with having to stand trial even if they themselves had not been part of the drug business. In order to get the interviewees to cooperate, the police used this threat or actually arrested the women, hoping that this would force the men to talk. They promised to let the girlfriend or wife go free if the men informed. Referring to a law that regulated custody of children,[5] the police could upgrade their threats: "If both of you are arrested, you cannot be considered suitable as parents."

"Most of us just lie around. We refuse to talk. We just wait for the time to pass. We know our rights, and they gotta have proof that will stand up in court. Nothing else ever worked before (referring to his own situation). . . . But now they've got the woman and the kid, and are talking 'bout custody rights, and so on. . . ."

In another example, the police used yet another, more concrete means of playing on immediate emotions, according to a young drug dealer:

"Nobody believes there's torture in Sweden, but there is. I was put in the cell next to hers [his girlfriend] so I would hear her weeping every day. Every goddam day I heard her weeping. For two months. Daily. I was about to. . . . It was to soften me up. She begged me the whole time to tell the truth. At last I had to. I didn't want to lose her and the kid."

The problem of getting caught between the loyalties to one's partners in crime and one's family did not present a difficult moral conflict for most. To choose the family seemed almost self-evident. For one of the men, however, it did constitute a problem. Not surprisingly his identity was still that of a thief, which was what he wanted to be. The reason for his ambivalence might be the fact that the woman for whose sake he had informed had left him. At the time of the interview, he stated that he genuinely regretted having "cooperated" but also said that he had seen no alternative at the time but to inform in order to save his former girl friend.

A third way of avoiding the designation of "snitch" is by invoking a higher loyalty. (Prus 1975; Navasky 1982) Using this argument one claims that the social typing is premature or subject to alternative interpretations. In the current example, among those known as informers, one invoked norms that took precedence over the norm "you shall not inform." One example is the argument for saving the family. Another is the use of an alternative moral system. This applies in the case of the one interviewee who was a Scientologist. When he got caught, this group became more important to him than it had been before. To make a statement against his former drug-centered group thus became something of a symbolic action affirming his real loyalties.

"I testified because I'd been in Scientology before. I wanted to come back in again, and knew I couldn't without admitting total responsibility."
"They demanded that?"
"Yeah, you could say that. Not 'them,' but it's required for you yourself, you could say."

An interesting variant of "invoking a higher loyalty" that we heard about from the prison staff was when inmates informed because they thought that this would be in the interest of the whole collective. The warden of one prison told us of an example in which one prisoner who was highly respected by the other inmates informed about a few who planned an escape. The reason for his telling was that the escape plans involved the use of violence. He feared that this would result in more controls and stricter rules for those who stayed behind.

The denial of injury, that is, a denial of the causal efficacy of the action, is an argument that emphasizes the consequences of the discredited behavior. (Sykes and Matza 1957) When the interviewees used this type of defense, they claimed that more than enough information had already been obtained by the police. One inmate, who stated that the police "knew anyhow" because before he was questioned they had already acquired evidence in the form of drugs or photos of people making a deal, emphasized that his information made no difference one way or the other: "We had too much evidence against us. Even if all of us had kept our mouths shut, it wouldn't have mattered." ("We" were said to be thirteen – ten who talked and three who did not.)

Several of the interviewees also claimed that someone else had already informed the police so it did not matter if one more person did as well. It is believed that refusing to talk in this situation would just have made matters worse for oneself by getting a longer sentence without any benefit to anyone else. A refusal to inform would just be a defiant gesture with nothing to gain and a lot to lose.

Challenging the Designating Agent

By using this form of tactic, the target is "rejecting the rejectors" (Sykes and Matza 1957), or "condemning the condemners" as McCorkle and Korn (1954), chose to call it. This is done in various ways.

First, the most common strategy – all interviewees used it, in fact – was what Goffman (1963) has called questioning the normals. Most stigmatized groups or individuals question whether the normals really are as blameless as they present themselves. One example of the reasoning behind this was expressed by a prisoner in this way: "There's not a single police investigation, not one drug case, without things getting told, 'cause if nothing was said to the police no one would ever do time except those caught in the act."

In our interviews both snitches and nonsnitches claimed that most criminals (some said 70–80 percent) snitch at one time or another. Using these figures, we can readily understand the applicability of the normalizing strategy: one's own informing can be seen as more of an accident than as a result of a real or unusual "crime" being discovered. Legitimizations of this kind are often followed by statements that those who are most active in harassing snitches do so because they have bad consciences themselves – they do it as a cover-up: "Often those who scream the most in the pen are those who squealed the most – so you won't question them."

The majority of the interviewed snitches were involved in drug-related cases. It is possible that the belief that "almost everybody has snitched" is true in this type of case. There are two reasons for this. First, drug cases often involve many individuals. The more links in a chain, the greater the chance that one of the links will break One reason is that the police have more than one or two people to pressure. Further, from the informer's point of view they might believe it is more difficult for other associates involved to know who snitched. Second, the police have a greater incentive to use informers in drug cases than in many others since they are considered as victimless crimes. Therefore it can be assumed that the police try harder to produce more informers in a case where drugs are involved particularly as it currently is considered prestigious to solve these cases. (Hansen 1984)

Drug cases involving many people also seem to produce informer chains; that is, if one person reveals something, the police then use this information as a lever on the next person, who might then divulge a bit more, and so on. If one is made a link in the informer chain, the feeling of guilt can be diminished by this knowledge or belief. An example is this statement: "They confessed to their own crimes. Then they nailed other people, so they're not one bit better than me."

Most addicts tend to take it for granted that "drugs make you snitch," that if you are addicted, you can't help but behave "immorally." "You are so sick from withdrawal after a few days in the slammer, that you cannot resist the police's persuasion." This is coupled with a belief that addicts are generally demoralized; they do not have any sense of solidarity. This is said to be present in acts other than informing, such as when stealing from friends. It is also a belief that can function to diminish personal guilt.

Another way of defusing the accusers' claims is through nihilation, a concept that Berger and Luckmann (1972) use to describe the process aimed at making invalid the moral claims of groups competing about the "right" way of acting and thinking. This strategy requires informers to deny that the statement from the accusers is legitimate. Many of those staying in the protected wards talked with great contempt about those on the ordinary wards. They were often seen as simple, typical criminals. By looking down on them with contempt, their importance and that of their judgments are reduced.[6] An example was given by a former marijuana dealer who served part of his sentence in a protected ward:

"I'd probably put myself in voluntary isolation just to get away from the others. I think they're sick. Even if they'd left me alone, I wouldn't hang out with'em. I'd rather have isolated myself and lie down and read a good book. Hang out with some. . . . Rather hanging out with a squealer [in isolation], a calm, sensible person, than with two, or three idiots from down there. I don't like that kinda person. I don't like the way they think, the way they live."

One interesting form of explanation is the use of arguments derived from the norm system of the group that has made the accusations, in this case the norms of the criminals. Here one is, so to say, arguing from inside the group. Such an example was found in an argument referring to the individual-responsibility model among criminals. The belief in individual responsibility is generally strong in Western cultures, but seems in some way to be even more so among criminals. (Shover 1971; Letkemann 1973; Åkerström 1985a) One argues that one should be prepared to accept the consequences of one's actions; that is, "if you wanna' play, you gotta' pay" or "If you can't do the time, don't do the crime." It is furthermore one's own responsibility if one gets caught. One example of using this value of being prepared for "paying for one's crime" is this:

". . . the court sentences me and I'm doing time for it. And. . . the big man, I mean, he knew what to expect when he got involved in the game. So he can't blame me if he got eight years. It ain't my fault."

Resisting by Relocation

This tactic can be defined as "leaving the scene." Targets seek out new audiences separated from the old ones by communicative (physical or social) or ideological distance. Defining oneself as a nonmember seems to be one of the most effective ways of alleviating guilt. Since snitching implies an act of treachery to an in-group, the label is not applicable to nonmembers. If you are in the process of changing your life-style and are converted by therapy or religion, testifying is sometimes defined as a choosing of sides. One example of this attitude is evident in a statement by the inmate who was a member of the church of Scientology:

"I got rid of all mine. . . .I took responsibility for myself, and wanted to straighten out, so I decided to do it . . . and it doesn't allow other interests."
"You testified against others?"

"Yeah . . . it ain't generally accepted, to put it mildly, in prisons . . . and that I can understand. It's obvious, it's a group and must be supported. There are two sides, see. Either you go over to one or you stay in the other. So against *that* group it's kind of treachery."

In some drug rehabilitation programs that are not religious, distancing through witnessing against former companions is actually demanded or at least encouraged as a "method." To explain informing on grounds such as these is something that is met with little understanding among other inmates. The moral validity of this stance – "to take a stand" – has been brought up and questioned spontaneously by inmates in the nonprotected wards because they believe it is possible to start fresh without putting old friends in jail.

In the game model, one uses "the game" as a frame of reference and thus enters a bargaining relation instead of having one's loyalties to the criminal group as a guiding perspective. This attitude can be described as an "each-man-for-himself-philosophy." Commenting on the relations between addicts as informers and the police, Lidz and Walker (1980, 154) note:

> It is worth reiterating here that the "game" conceptualization of cop-addict interaction was an important resource for the detectives trying to "turn on" a potential informant. To some degree, it neutralized the addict's view of himself as the noble outlaw. By being able to contend that "it's only a game," the detectives could try to direct the addict's attention to his own immediate situation and their contention that informing would be pragmatically justified.

There was only one interviewee in my study who, without any show of scruple or elaboration, told about his informing in this manner.[7] The situation he described is one in which he tried to make a deal with a guard because he was harassed by other inmates for failing to pay a debt. He is attempting to make an exchange: information for a transfer:

"Have you any good tips to give me?" So I said to him that we could make a deal. "Yeah, that's what we are interested in," he said. "Who has horse? [heroin]," he asked me. "I didn't find it." – If I can get out of here, I told him . . . .

The others who – even if not in such a straightforward way – had adopted this way of viewing their informing, expressed their attitude as "one has to give and take" in life when talking about the interrogation situation. Another sign of using this perspective was the frequent disappointment with the outcome of informing on the part of those interviewed, even if no promises had been made by the police or the prosecutor. The informers clearly expected something in return – at least being protected afterwards. This was something the authorities often did not accomplish. The feeling of unfairness that resulted might in part have replaced the question of whether their own informing was justified or not. One example of someone who was harassed at the prison where he was staying and complained that the authorities did not help him transfer to a safer institution follows:

"The question is what's their deal. I've helped them, now they should help me."
"Have you got nothing in return for. . . ?"
"Not shit."
"Were you promised anything?"
"No, but still. . . ."

Discussion

Among the interviewed informers several major forms for counteracting the label of snitch were seen: "Challenging the designation" with the subcategories of using euphemisms, disavowing responsibility, invoking a higher loyalty, and denial of injury. Another was "challenging the designating agent," which consisted of questioning the normal's morality, nihilation, and using the norm of individual responsibility emphasized by criminals. Finally, "resisting by relocation" consisted of defining oneself as a nonmember, and shifting one's focus to a game perspective when interacting with the police, thus neutralized one's relationship and loyalties to the criminal group.

The reason I used these forms suggested by Prus (1975) rather than any other analyses[8] is that he concentrates on individuals dealing with an immediate situation instead of a group striving to change its image over a period of time. The fact that the individual-centered approach was most applicable in analyzing informers is significant. I did not find any strategies that were collectively used.

One such collective tactic both commonly used and powerful in its consequences is the inversion of stigmas. (Taylor 1976; Rotenberg 1974) This is employed by those who, when labeled, totally embrace the role but place it in a vocabulary that inverts its original meaning. Words such as "gay" or slogans such as "black is beautiful" can thus be employed as banners in ideological campaigns. It is hard to imagine the same strategy used by informers.[9] In fact the common use of euphemisms among the interviewees, the avoidance of words as informers, snitches, and so on, is the very opposite of a strategy aimed at making a behavior or a group of people respectable.

The lack of a collective strategy can be viewed as the outcome of two characteristics. The first aspect concerns their status as individuals. Since the informer is viewed and treated as an atypical member of the group, he probably sees himself in this light. In addition, informing is mostly a hidden activity. Therefore, it would be extremely difficult for informers to acquire a social base or platform from which to advocate their cause even if they had a common one. Additionally, arguing their cause as a group could be met with little understanding since the very activity – betrayal – is directed against the larger group. In this they are much more directly a threat to a group than, say, homosexuals to heterosexuals.

The second aspect concerns the centrality of the role. Betrayal is a central issue, but unlike groups such as blacks and gays, informers do not share a common set of interests unless interest is defined in the narrow sense of hiding their betrayal and, if discovered, the desire for protection. They do not share a common history or even the idea that betraying in itself is something morally commendable. It has to be justified.

Notes

1. Not only the actors themselves but "interested parties" use a different vocabulary to attribute or resist this type of designation. While the inmates used words such as "finks," canaries," etc., the prison staff used the more neutral word: "witnesses" or that "someone had testified." Similarily in Navasky's (1982) study of the Hollywood informers during the McCarthy era, it is pointed out that while the left used words like "informers," "belly-crawlers," the Committee and the American legion used words like "friendly," or "cooperative."
2. The delicacy of the subject was evidenced in that most of the informers at the protected wards did not even tell other inmates at these wards the reason for their being there.
3. A few articles had conveniently just appeared in the newspapers on the subject.
4. Such shows of loyalty are perhaps not uncommon in contexts where the new is heavily contrasted with the old. To "take the stand" as a show of one's new loyalty was one of the arguments for former communists to witness against old fellow members in the party during the McCarthy era. One of the famous witnesses, Chambers, actually described informing as a self-cleansing process. (Navasky 1982)

5. What the police are said to do in this case is to threaten to notify the social authorities so that they will place the children in custody.
6. According to Lidz and Walker (1980), the police also use the arguments of this strategy while trying to recruit informers.
7. The reason for him adopting the game perspective might be due to the fact that it was easier for him as a gypsy to diminish the importance of loyalty to other criminals, in this case nongypsies. That is, the latter already constituted, at least in some respect, an out-group.
8. E.g., Goffman 1963; Taylor 1976; Rotenberg 1974.
9. Exceptions may always be found however. The McCarthy witness, Chambers, used the concept of informer in this way. This was not common among his "collegues" and it was not meant to be a defense for all informers, in all situations (whereas this is the case for gays and blacks).

7

Cronstedt: A Concluding Illustration

Sing not his rank, his kin ne'er name,
His crime must be his own;
May no one redden for the shame
That falls on him alone.
He who his native land betrays,
No father has, nor son, nor race.

The name "False Arm" shall him adorn,
For Finland's stay once placed;
Call him Dishonor, Shame, and Scorn,
And Death, by crime disgraced!
Thus only should his name appear,
To spare the ears of them that hear.

Take all the darkness of the grave,
And all the woes that live,
And build thereof a name for knave,
And him the title give;–
'Twould wake less sorrow evermore
Than name at Sveaborg he bore!

– J.L. Runeberg.
(From translation by Shaw 1925, 146–147)

These verses were chanted as a young girl started her first day at class by the school children. The young girl's name was Cronstedt and she bore the name that was not to be mentioned. Runeberg, who published these verses in the mid-nineteenth century, was a Finnish-Swedish national poet. He drove home his intention to insult by never mentioning the traitor's

131

name in his seventeen-verse poem "Sveaborg." Sveaborg was the most important Swedish stronghold when Finland still belonged to Sweden. In 1808 the Russians attacked Finland. Shortly after the outbreak of the war Sveaborg was surrendered to Russia, with hardly a shot fired by its commander, Admiral Carl Olof Cronstedt. This was said to have settled the war in Russia's favor. The quoted verses is part of *Ensign Stål's Songs* which was obligatory reading for school children until rather recently. The incident of the chanting in the classroom was told by a girl in that class, a grandmother of one of my friends, and it took place approximately a hundred years after the treachery itself.

I will use the example of Cronstedt to illustrate some of the themes discussed earlier in this book.

First of all, the chanting incident described above shows the centrality of betrayal as a social phenomenon. Not only was the traitor immortalized by a poem, but the memory of the incident was still alive a hundred years later.

"Cronstedt" in itself was furthermore so steeped with meaning that the mere name generated a reaction for generations. This seems to be a general tendency so that those associated with the betrayer – innocent or not – will be affected.[1] Parenthetically, the fact that names of well-known traitors are kept alive is significant. Some names do carry such general meanings, or become symbols for something else, such as Romeo and Juliet for love; Casanova for lust; and Brutus, Judas, and Quisling for treachery.

The case of Cronstedt moreover illustrates how the "third party" – those benefitting from the betrayal – joins in the contempt: "When Tzar Alexander had showed the convention of the 6th of April to the French Ambassador Caulaincourt, he said, What do you think of this Cronstedt, who gives his master's troops to me and proclaims Finland's surrender in advance?" (Hornborg 1955, 85)

Betrayal has been analyzed as an act directed against a We. This We may be a nation, work colleagues, or a family. This means that each individual is a member of several We's at the same time, which may make conflicting demands for one's loyalty. Cronstedt was caught in such a situation. When Sveaborg was attacked, many civilians had fled there for protection. Among the civilians who lived in the fort were Cronstedt's own wife and children, a fact which could not have encouraged him to fight to the last man.[2]

Betrayal has been viewed (in this book) as a normal and common social phenomenon. The Cronstedt case is uncommon and dramatic. Even in such contexts, however, the common or ordinary is relevant. Here it can be seen in the chanting incident and also in the fact that betrayal often presents itself as a choice of whom to betray – in this case the family or the nation.

The many social forms and strategies for avoiding treachery have been noted. One of the interesting ways to avoid betrayal is not to show distrust according to Luhmann (1979), who describes a process of distrust breeding distrust. Sveaborg was not considered an attractive posting and Cronstedt was posted there after a conflict with the king, which might have eased his decision not to fight. This might explain why Cronstedt was influenced by those who argued for a capitulation: "Cronstedt, who was already bitter towards the King and sceptical of the war, listened, hesitated, wavered and fell!" (*Svenska Dagbladet*/Swedish Daily/ August 2, 1987, p. 24)

Cronstedt also illustrates the uses of labeling someone a betrayer. His betrayal not only "explained" the outcome of the war, but also provided a scapegoat: "Sveaborgs capitulation was a complete shock for the Swedes. 'The Gibraltar of the North' was supposed to be impregnable, or so it was said. The one who became the whipping boy for that national disgrace was Cronstedt." (*Svenska Dagbladet*/ September 4, 1987, p. 17, part II)

Betrayal is no lighthearted matter, done without need for justification. The admiral presented his *Apologia* in his book "Sanna upplysningar angående orsaker, som gifvit anledning till den emellan f.d. Viceamiralen och Kommedanten på Sveaborgs fästning och Kejserl. Ryske Gener. Suchtelen den 6 april 1808 slutna Conventionen." (Translated: True information concerning causes which led to the convention signed on April 6, 1808 by the former Vice Admiral and Commander of Sveaborg Fort and the Imperial Russian General Suchtelen." [Stockholm 1811])

The reactions to his explanations show (in general) that no excuses are acceptable. Those who condemn him first present his arguments and then attack them. To declare that one was fooled is no excuse. The Russians fooled the Swedes by pretending that their attacking army was greater than it was and that other countries were now attacking Sweden. Cronstedt was isolated and could not get information from Sweden. This is not a defensible argument, since one is not supposed to be easily taken in: "The Russians were damnably clever at fooling Cronstedt, and he was damnably easy to fool." (*Svenska Dagbladet, Ibid.*) Nor are the other explanations acceptable: lack of gun powder, lack of food, untrained soldiers, etc. Whether he thought a defense was pointless or not is irrelevant. The respected Finnish historian Hornborg wrote:

Naturally the arguments Cronstedt later presented in defending his actions were purely and simply shams. His real motives are only of some psychological interest . . . that he committed treason is not even up for discussion. He had been entrusted with the stoutest stronghold in the kingdom, he had accepted commission of trust, and he had – for no objective reason – let everyone down. Not even a royal decree – if such a thing were within the realm of possibility – could have authorized him to give up the stronghold and give away the fleet. (1955, 86; my translation.)

So far a picture of betrayal as a central issue and the betrayer as despised by all has been presented. In spite of this, one often finds exceptions to the rule, circumstances that may strengthen or loosen the labeling; such negotiations, mitigating circumstances, and context-dependent factors have been considered important to distinguish. A few of them will be discussed.

The historian quoted above, Hornborg, was, for example, ready to accept betrayal in the form of disobedience to the king as long as Cronstedt did not betray his country. In fact, he was regretful that some of the officers did not remove Cronstedt when it became clear that capitulation was intended. Thus, at times betrayal is acceptable.

It was also said that the "third party" shares the contempt, even when the betrayal is useful for them. Yet, in some instances the third party may applaud the betrayer. One often hear regrets about how hard it is to prove and correct problems and faults in some occupations because those who are aware of the problem are bound by feelings of loyalty and feel obliged to cover up for others in the We. Those who tell anyhow, sometimes called "whistleblowers," may even acquire a hero status among those benefitting from the information. "Whistleblower" is an interesting example of the importance of language in the evaluation of betrayers. Although this is one of the positive "etiquettes" for betrayers, the association to precisely this makes one commentator campaign for a better word: ethical resister.[3] The moral battleground is evidenced in many contexts where betrayal is an issue: one is either a collaborator or a realist, a cooperative witness or an informer, etc. Language, or the choice of words, can actually be seen as a tool when attempts are made by the third party to lessen or redefine the images of betrayers.

Another exception from the rule of basic and long-lasting contempt is the fact that betrayers, at least well-known ones, often become subjects for a recurring moral evaluation and redefinition. In the same way that contempt can last for a long time, so can defenders present their versions of the betrayal long after the act took place:

Vice Admiral Cronstedt was perhaps not the cowardly wretch that we have been taught to believe. . . . "Furthermore the fabled stronghold was poorly built," says an amateur historian, Hanns Heinz Ollus, who has taken it upon himself to rewrite the accepted version of the story surrounding the traitor Carl Olof Cronstedt. (*Svenska Dagbladet*, September 4, 1989, p. 1, part II)

This reevaluation is not restricted to Cronstedt; it appears to be quite common. Not all betrayers are reevaluated of course, but those well known for their treason or who are famous for other reasons, are often the subject of many such discussions. Notabilities such as Errol Flynn, Wodehouse, Leander, and Hergé have been discussed in this manner.[4] Among those simply known as traitors, even Judas has been the object of similar discussion. Some claim he should not be seen as a traitor – his role had to be filled and he happened to be its executor. Since Jesus had to be betrayed, Judas was simply following the script. (Hellesnes 1978)

Neither Cronstedt nor Judas can hardly be said to be traitors only through a social construction. But Wodehouse can be said to be and his is an interesting example as it illuminates the tendency not only to equal treachery with acts meant to harm the We. Wodehouse's betrayal consisted of making a radio speech from Berlin during the war. His speech was a causerie about his own experiences of prison camp life and certainly not propaganda for the Germans. Still, he was seen as fraternizing with Them. To this was added the fact that he was released soon after the program; it was interpreted as a part of a deal while in fact the date was decided before he agreed to broadcast. It was more or less accidentally that this came to be seen as treacherous, as it was dependent on a few persons' initiatives – hardly anyone in Britain had listened to the program. (Usborne 1988) Since he himself had been interned for a year, he could hypothetically have ended up with a halo instead of being stigmatized. Furthermore, his case shows the dynamite in such a label – he never returned to England.

Some complications have been adressed in this book, while others have not. One of the unexplored but interesting phenomenon is the fact that sometimes, as in the case of Cronstedt, the betrayal remained in peoples' minds for more than century. At other times, however, time actually heals the wound.

Lottman (1986, 164) comments on the effectiveness of French collaborators who hid for a considerable time after World War II. In relation to a publisher of a well-known collaboration newspaper, who was tried after years of hiding, he quotes *L'Humanité* : ". . . Horace de Carbuccia has finally been acquitted. What else could have been done with him? His editor Henri Béraud was sentenced to death. But that was ten years ago!" (Paris, October 20, 1955)

Notes

1. The coloring off of a label can also go the other way. Lottman (1986) gives one example of how someone suspected of being a collaborator was freed because he was a relative of someone in the Resistance. This tendency of a reputation that includes others is obviously not restricted to relatives. Those surrounded with a trust capital can vouch for someone suspected and at times can free them. This is also evident in Lottman's description of the purge in France where many intellectuals, who were known to be active in the Resistance "saved" suspects.
2. *Bra Böckers Lexikon* and *Svenska Dagbladet*/Swedish daily/, September 4, 1987.
3. Golembiewski writes in a review of books on whistleblowers: "I find the term whistleblower repugnant . . . . The term does rise above some related usages – e.g., rat, snitch, stool pigeon – but not much." (1989, 91)
4. A discussion of whether the Swedish singer and actress Zarah Leander was a traitor in the sense of being friendly towards the Nazis has been kept alive ever since she worked in Germany during the war. In a newspaper comment about her in connection with some films and musicals, it was said, "Zarah's brown period has been a topic for discussion ever since she returned to Sweden in 1942. . . . A little less than a year ago, a great Zarah debate broke out in connection with two musicals . . . something new was presented: Nils Berman showed a sort of statement which was supposed to exonerate Zarah. Berman . . . was the friend who helped Mrs. Leander make a come back in 1949, after a 7-year ban. He has found among his papers one in which an American agent feels that she is on our side. The battle about Zarah's disputed closeness to the Nazi leaders never ends." (*Expressen* /Swedish daily/ December 28, 1988)

    For similar comments on Hergé: "The issue of Hergé's own politics remains a contentious one even six years after his death. He was branded a collaborator after the Second World War for working for a pro-German newspaper and a recent article in *Time Out* magazine ran the headline "Was Tintin a Nazi?" (*Economist*, August 26, 1989, 86)

    The moral evaluation can also consist of correcting false information, as with Errol Flynn, as this feature writer describes: "Several years ago, some b-st-rd author published a book labeling Errol Flynn a Nazi spy. Robin Hood – a traitor! Captain Blood would have collaborated with the Japs. The Sea Hawk secretly having admired Adolf Hitler. . . . The author claimed he could prove his claims as he had found some old notes at the FBI. He must be more than a little off his rocker, 'cause how can you compare a note in the FBI's files with the last scenes in 'Robin Hood'? But we weren't so perspicacious when that damned book came out and and spread its heresies. These revolting accusations affected a whole generation like a nail through the soul . . . (but) recently Winston Churchill's security Advisor Sir William Stephenson revealed that Errol Flynn did supply the Germans with secret info during WW II. But it was information that he handed over under the direction of the English MI-5. Captain Blood was in reality a secret agent for the British. Robin Hood tricked the Germans. The Sea Hawk was a real hero. Just like we always thought!" (*Sydsvenska Dagbladet* /Swedish daily/ February 12, 1989, p. 4, part 3)

Appendix
Method and Sample of the Study of Criminal Informers

The analyses of criminal informers originated from a study of violence and threats in Swedish prisons conducted in 1983 and 1984. (Åkerström 1985) Although some quantitative data were gathered from interrogation transcripts, it was considered so unreliable that the main data were based on in-depth, tape-recorded interviews. The sample consisted of onehundred and four inmates (ninety-four men, ten women). Interviews were also conducted with forty-one persons from the prison staff on various levels in the hierarchy. The reason for interviewing so many, usually judged unnecessary in a qualitative study, was to compare different institutions.

Those who were known to be or described themselves as informers comprised twenty-three male interviewees. Of the twenty-three, eight claimed to be innocently accused of this "crime." Those defined as informers were more often involved in drug cases than the rest of the group.

The interviewees were located at nine different prisons (about half in high-security ones and half in smaller, more open ones) in Sweden. About two-thirds of the interviewed inmates were found in wards for those who themselves asked to be "isolated" or "semi-isolated." Some of these wards contained totally isolated cells, but most were wards where the prisoners could socialize during part of the day. These wards were cut off from the rest of the prison, however.

The interviewees were all men. Some requested transfers to these wards because they preferred a drug-free environment or simply wished to stay in calmer surroundings than the normal wards. Most of them wanted to be there because they had been harassed by other prisoners. The reasons for this harassment included having failed to pay one's debts to other inmates, or having committed particularly heinous crimes in the opinions of the other inmates such as sex offenses or beating or killing one's wife, girl friend, or children, or being labeled an informer.

All the inmates were asked questions about informers. Since the study was of an exploratory kind, the questions were unstructured. Each interview took between one and two hours, and some prisoners were interviewed twice.

The setting where the interviews were conducted was either in the cells of the inmates or in the visitors' rooms. They were always held in private, on a one-to-one basis and the inmates were promised and given as much anonymity as was possible. We made a point of not asking for names, age, nationality (if not Swedish), etc. I would judge that the inmates were of average "inmate age" (around twenty-five) and most were Swedes, although a few were foreigners, mainly from Southern Europe. The crimes the interviewees had committed represented those in the ordinary prison population (mostly thefts and/or drug-related crimes).   Some had, however, committed robberies, murders, sex offenses, or tax frauds.

The interviews were conducted by three graduate students in sociology, one of whom had himself spent time in prison, and by me. We presented ourselves as researchers from a university. Evidence of rapport could be seen in us being told by some inmates about their having informed though they had managed to keep that a secret from other inmates. We were also – quite often – told about illegalities and the breaking of rules in prison; information we would not have been given, had we been seen as potential snitches.

Bibliography

Adams, S. 1984. *Roche versus Adams*. London: Cape.

Agar, M. H. 1980. *The Professional Stranger*. New York: Academic Press.

Allbeury, T. 1981. *The Other Side of Silence*. New York: Granada.

Åkerström, M. 1985a. *Crooks and Squares - lifestyles of thieves and addicts in comparison to conventional people*. New Brunswick, N. J.: Transaction Books.

_____. 1985b. *Våld och hot bland intagna i kriminalvårdsanstalt*. Norrköping: Kriminalvårdsstyrelsen.

_____. 1987. *Kvinnor i verkstan?* Lund: Department of Sociology, University of Lund.

_____. 1988. "Att offra sig för offren." In *Brottsoffer*. Stockholm: Brottsförebyggande rådet.

Andenaes, J., O. Riste, and M. Skodvin, eds. 1966. *Norway and the Second World War*. Oslo: Tanum.

Ash, T. G. 1985. "Espionage Among Friends - A Master Spy But Not A Traitor." *New Republic* 193, 13-15.

Asplund, J. 1987. *Det sociala livets elementära former*. Göteborg: Korpen.

Aubert, V. 1965. "Secrecy: the Underground as a Social System." In Aubert, V. *The Hidden Society*. pp. 288-310. Totowa, N.J.: The Bedminster Press.

Bailey, F., ed. 1971. *Gifts and Poisons: the Politics of Reputation*. Oxford: Blackwell.

Barnes, 1979. *Who Should Know What? Social Science, Privacy and Ethics*. Harmonsworth: Penguin.

Bateson, G. 1977. "From Versailles to Cybernetics." In *Steps to an Ecology of Mind*. pp. 469-477. New York: Ballantine.

Beck, F. and W. Godin. [pseudonyms] 1951. *Russian Purge and the Extraction of Confession*. London: Hurst & Blackett Ltd.

Becker, H. 1960. "Notes on the Concept of Commitment." *American Journal of Sociology* LXVI,32-40.

_____. 1963. *Outsiders - Studies in the Sociology of Deviance*. New York: Free Press.

Bentley, E., ed. 1971. *Thirty Years of Treason - Excerpts from Hearings before the House Committee on Un-American Activities, 1938-1968*. New York: Viking Press.

Berger, P. 1963. *Invitation to Sociology - A Humanistic Perspective*. Garden City, N.Y.: Anchor Books.

Berger, P. and Luckmann, T. 1972. *The Social Construction of Reality*. London: Penguin University Books.

Bjorneboe, J. 1971. "Svikeren." In *Norge, mitt Norge*. Oslo: Pax.

141

Blum, H. 1987. *I Pledge Allegiance - the True Story of the Walkers: An American Spy Family.* New York: Simon and Schuster.

Board of Trustees, National Council on Crime and Delinquency. 1972. "The Use of Juveniles as Informers in Drug-Abuse Matters." *Crime and Delinquency* 18, 129-130.

Bok, S. 1982. *Secrets: On the Ethics of Concealment and Revelation.* New York: Pantheon.

Bondeson, U. 1974. *Fången i Fångsamhället.* Malmö: Norstedts.

Bowker, L. 1977. *Prisoner Subcultures.* Lexington: Lexington Books.

____. 1980. *Prisoner Victimization.* New York: Elsevier.

Braconier, F. 1989. *Som vi behagar - svensk neutralitetspolitik från Napoleonkrigen till EG.* Stockholm: Timbro.

Bratt, I. 1988. *Mot rädslan.* Stockholm: Carlsson.

Bulmer, M. 1980. "Comment on 'The Ethics of Covert Methods'." *British Journal of Sociology* 31, 59-65.

Caplow, T. 1968. *Two Against One - Coalitions in Triads.* Englewood Cliffs, N.J.: Prentice Hall.

Case, C. 1987. "Deviance as a Rational Response: Disguise, Deceit, and Conspiracy among Racehorse Trainers." *Deviant Behavior* 8, 329-342.

Cawelti, J. and B. Rosenberg. 1987. *The Spy Story.* Chicago and London: University of Chicago Press.

Chafee, Z., Jr. 1952. "Spies into Heroes." *The Nation* 174, 618-619.

Clemmer, D. 1940. *The Prison Community.* New York: Holt, Rinehart & Winston.

Coleman, J. 1975. *Addiction, Crime and Abstinence.* Ph.D. diss. Santa Barbara: University of California.

Cookridge, E. 1966. *Inside S.O.E.* London: Arthur Barker.

Coser, L. 1974. *Greedy Institutions - Patterns of Undivided Commitment.* New York: Free Press.

Cottle, T. 1980. *Children's Secrets.* Garden City, N.Y.: Doubleday.

Cressey, D. 1953. *Other People's Money.* New York: Free Press.

____. 1977. *Theft of the Nation.* New York: Harper Torchbooks.

Davis, M. 1973. *Intimate Relations.* New York: Free Press.

Denning, M. 1987. *Cover Stories: Narrative and Ideology in the British Spy Thriller.* London, New York: Routledge and Kegan Paul.

Donner, F. J. 1954. "The Informer." *The Nation* April 10. 178, 298-309.

____. 1973. "Political Informers." In *Investigating the FBI*, eds. P. Watters, and S. Gillers. New York: Doubleday.

Driver, E. D. 1970. "Confessions and the Social Psychology of Coercion." In *Law and Order in a Democratic Society*, edited by M. Summers and T. Barth. Columbus, Ohio: Charles E. Merrill.

Durkheim, E. (1895) 1964. *The Rules of Sociological Method.* New York: Free Press.

____. (1915) 1965. *The Elementary Forms of the Religious Life.* New York: Free Press.

____. 1983. *Durkheim and the Law*, edited by S. Lukes And A. Scull. Oxford: Martin Robertson.

Erikson, K. 1966. *Wayward Puritans - A Study in the Sociology of Deviance.* London: Wiley.

Farge, Y. 1946. *Rebelles, Soldats et Citoyens.* Paris: B. Grasset.

Ferraro, K. 1983. "Negotiating Trouble in a Battered Women's Shelter." *Urban Life* 12, 287-306.

Finkelhor, D. 1987. "Trauma of Child Sexual Abuse." *Journal of Interpersonal Violence* 2, 348-366.

Fitzgerald, E. 1989 *The Pentagonists - An Insider's View of Waste, Mismanagement, and Fraud in Defense Spending*. Boston: Houghton Mifflin.

Forster, E. M. 1972. *Two Cheers for Democracy*. New York: Harcourt.

Galbraith, J. K. 1977. "Humble Quislings." *The New Republic* July 2, 177, 7.

Garbus, M. 1987. *Traitors and Heroes - a Lawyer's Memoir*. New York: Atheneum.

Giallombardo, R. 1966. *Society of Women: a Study of Womens' Prison*. New York: Wiley.

Glaser, D. 1969. *The Effectiveness of a Prison and Parole System*. New York: Bobbs-Merrill.

Goffman, E. 1959. *The Presentation of Self in Everyday Life*. New York: Anchor Books.

_____. 1963. *Stigma - Notes on the Management of Spoiled Identity*. Englewood Cliffs, N.J.: Prentice Hall.

_____. 1969. *Where the Action Is*. New York: Penguin, Allen Lane.

_____. 1972. *Relations in Public - Microstudies of the Public Order*. New York: Harper Torchbooks.

_____. 1982. *Interaction ritual - Essays on Face-to-Face Behavior*. New York: Pantheon Books.

_____. 1986. *Frame Analysis - An Essay on the Organization of Experience*. Boston: Northeastern University Press.

Goode, W. J. 1978. *The Celebration of Heroes - Prestige as a Control System*. Berkeley: University of California Press.

Golembiewski, R. 1989 Bookreview. Fitzgerald, The Pentagonist and Glazer & Glazer, The Whistleblowers, *Society* 26, 6, 90-93.

Gosling, J. 1959. *The Ghost Squad*. London: W. H. Allen.

Gouldner, H. and M. Symons Strong. 1987. *Speaking of Friendship - Middle Class Women and Their Friends*. New York: Greenwood Press.

Grenier, R. 1985. "Treason Chic." *Commentary* 79, 61-65.

Griffiths and Ayers. 1967. "A Postscript to the Miranda Project: Interrogation of Draft Protestors." *Yale Law Journal* 77, 300-319.

Gross, E. and G. P. Stone. 1974. "Embarassment and the Analysis of Role Requirements." In *People in Places - the Sociology of the Familiar*, eds. A. Birenbaum and E. Sagarin, pp. 101-120. New York: Praeger.

Gullestad, M. 1984. *Kitchen-Table Society*. Oslo: Universitetforlaget.

Hansen, J. 1984. *Okonventionella spaningsmetoder*. Unpubl. manuscript. Lund: Department of Sociology. University of Lund.

Harney, M. L. and J. C. Cross. 1960. *The Informer in Law Enforcement*. Springfield. Ill.: Charles C. Thomas.

Haugen, I. 1983. "Til sladerens pris - eller: om å vaere prisgitt sladderen." *Sosiologi idag* 4, 39-58.

Hayes, P. 1971. *Quisling - the Career and Political Ideas of Vidkun Quisling 1887-1945*. Newton Abbot: David & Charles.

Hellesnes, J. 1978. *Jakta etter svikaren - om nodvendet av praktisk filosofi*. Oslo: Gyldendal.

Hepworth, M. 1975. *Blackmail - Publicity and Secrecy in Everyday Life*. London and Boston: Routledge & Kegan Paul.

Hepworth, M. and B. Turner. 1982. *Confessions - Studies in Deviance and Religion*. London: Routledge & Kegan Paul.

Holm, P. 1951. *Bevingade Ord*. Stockholm: Bonniers.

Homan, R. 1980. "The Ethics of Covert Methods." *British Journal of Sociology* 31, 46-59.

Hornborg, E. 1955. *När riket sprängdes*. Stockholm: Norstedts.

Hughes, E. C. 1960. "Introduction: The Place of Field Work in Social Science." In *Field Work*, ed. B. Junker, pp. v-x. Chicago: University of Chicago Press.

____. 1984. *The Sociological Eye - Selected Papers*. New Brunswick, N.J.: Transaction Books.

Hugo, P. 1978. *Quislings or Realists - Documentary Study of Colored Politics in South Africa*. Johannesburg.

Ianni, F. A. J. 1972. *A Family Business*. New York: Russell Sage.

Inbau, F. E. and Reid, J. E. 1962. *Criminal Interrogation and Confessions*. Baltimore: Williams & Wilkins.

Irving, B. and L. Hilgendorf. 1980. *Police Interrogation*, and *A Case Study of Current Practice*. Research Studies No. 1. and No. 2. London: Royal Commission on Criminal Procedure.

James, C. H. 1975. *Silas Deane - Patriot or Traitor*. East Lansing: Michigan State University Press.

Johnson, E. 1961. "Sociology of Confinement: Assimilation and the Prison 'rat'." *The Journal of Criminology, Criminal Law, and Police Science* 51, 528-533.

Johnson, J. 1975. *Doing Field Research*. New York: Free Press.

Junker, B. H. 1960. *Field Work - An Introduction to Social Sciences*. Chicago: University of Chicago.

Katz, J. 1977. "Cover-Up and Collective Integrity: on the Natural Antagonisms of Authority Internal and External to Organizations." *Social Problems* 25, 3-17.

____. 1979. "Concerted Ignorance - The Social Construction of Cover-Up." *Urban Life* 8, 295-316.

King, R. D. 1989. "Treason and Traitors." *Society* July/August:39-48.

Klapp, O. 1964. *Symbolic Leaders, Public Dramas, and Public Men*. Chicago: Aldine.

____. 1971. *Social Types: Process, Structure, and Ethos*. San Diego: Aegis.

Klockars, C. 1974. *The Professional Fence*. London: Tavistock.

____. 1984a. "Introduction." *American Behavioral Scientist* 24, 413-422.

____. 1984b. "Blue Lies and Police Placebos - the Moralities of Police Lying." *American Behavioral Scientist* 24, 529-544.

Kogon, E. 1989. *SS Staten - De tyska koncentrationslägrens system*. (Original: Der SS-Staat - das System der Deutschen Konzentrationslager.) Stockholm: Berghs.

Lawson, A. 1988. *Adultery - An Analysis of Love and Betrayal*. New York: Basic Books.

Le Roy Ladurie, E. 1980. *Montaillou*. London: Penguin.

Lenin, V.I. (1902) 1929. "What Is To Be Done?" In *Collected Works*, IV, bk. II. New York: International Publishers.

Levinson, S 1983 "Under Cover: the Hidden Costs of Infiltration." In *ABSCAM Ethics*, edited by Caplan, G. New York: Ballinger.

Letkemann, P. 1973. *Crime as Work*. Englewood Cliffs, N.J.: Prentice Hall.

Levi, P. 1988. *The Drowned and the Saved*. Michael Joseph.

Lidz, C. and A. Walker. 1980. *Heroin, Deviance and Morality*. London: Sage.

Littlejohn, D. 1972. *The Patriotic Traitors: A History of Collaboration in German-Occupied Europe, 1940-1945*. London: Heinemann.

Lottman, H. R. 1985. *Pétain: Hero or traitor?* New York: Viking.

____. 1986. *The People's Anger - Justice and Revenge in Post-Liberation France*. London: Hutchinson.

Luhmann, N. 1979. *Trust and Power*. New York: Wiley.

Lundberg, S. 1989. *Flyktingskap - Latinamerikansk exil i Sverige och Västeuropa*. Lund: Arkiv.

Maas, P. 1970. *The Valachi Papers*. London: Panther.

____. 1973. *Serpico - the Cop Who Defied the System*. New York: Viking Press.

MacKenzie, N., ed. 1967. *Secret Societies*. New York: Collier Books.

Maguire, M. 1982. *Burglary in a Dwelling*. London: Heinemann.

Mann, K. 1985. *Defending White-Collar Crime - A Portrait of Attorneys at Work*. New Haven and London: Yale University Press.

Manning, P. 1978. "Rules, Colleagues, and Situationally Justified Actions." In *Policing: A View From the Street*, edited by P. Manning. Santa Monica, Calif.: Goodyear.

Marquart, J. W. and J. B. Roebuck. 1985. "Prison Guards and 'Snitches' - Deviance Within a Total Institution." *The British Journal of Criminology* 25, 217-233.

Mars, G. 1983. *Cheats at Work - An Anthropology of Workplace Crime*. London: Counterpoint.

Martin, D. 1978. *Patriot or Traitor: The Case of General Mihailovitch*. Stanford, Calif.: Hoover Institution.

McBain, E. 1975. *Hail to the Chief*. New York: Random House.

McCaghy, C. 1968. "Drinking and Deviance Disavowal: The Case of Child Molestors." *Social Problems* 16, 43-49.

McCleery, R. 1960. "Communication Patterns as Bases of System of Authority and Power." In *Theoretical Studies in Social Organization of the Prison*, edited by R. Cloward et al, pp. 52-56. New York: Pamphlet.

McCorkle, L. and R. Korn. 1954. "Resocialization within Walls." *Annals of American Academy of Political and Social Science* 293, 88-98.

Milner, C. and R. Milner. 1972. *Black Players - the Secret World of Black Pimps*. Boston, Toronto: Little Brown.

Montanino, F. 1984. "Protecting the Federal Witness - Burying Past Life and Biography." *American Behavioral Scientist* 27, 501-528.

Morris, T. and P. Morris. 1963. *Pentonville: A Sociological Study of an English Prison*. London: Routledge.

Moszkiewiez, H. 1987. *Inside the Gestapo*. London: Sphere Books.

Naegele, K. 1958. "Friendship and Acquaintances: An Exploration of Some Social Distinctions." *Harvard Educational Review* 28, 232-252.

Navasky, V. 1982. *Naming Names*. London: John Calder.

New Larousse Encyclopedia of Mythology. 1959. Feltham: Hamlyn.

Noelle-Neumann, E. 1984. *The Spiral of Silence - Public Opinion - Our Social Skin*. Chicago: University of Chicago Press.

Nonet, P. and P. Selznick. 1978. *Law and Society in Transition - Toward a Responsive Law*. New York: Harper & Row.

Oscapella, E. 1980. "A Study of Informers in England." *Criminal Law Review*, March, 136-146.

Paine, R. 1970. "Informal Communication and Information-Management." *Canadian Review of Sociology and Anthropology* 7, 172-188.

Penrose, B. and S. Freeman. 1987. *Conspiracy of Silence - the Secret Life of Anthony Blunt*. London: Grafton Books.

Pepper, A. 1979. *Straight Life*. New York: Schirmar Books.

Peters, E. 1988. *Inquisition*. New York: Free Press; London: Collier Macmillan.

Peterson, J. 1984. "Promises, Compromises, and Commitments - The Protection of Confidential Research Data." *American Behavioral Scientists* 24, 453-480.

Philbrick, H. 1952. *I led 3 Lives*. London: Hamish Hamilton.

Philby, E. 1968. *Kim Philby - the Spy I Loved*. London: Hamish Hamilton.

Philby, K. 1968. *My Silent War*. New York: Grove Press.

Pileggi, N. 1985. *Wise Guy*. London: Corgi Books.

Pincher, C. 1987. *Traitors - the Labyrinths of Treason*. London: Sidgwick & Jackson.

Pollner, M. and R. Emerson. 1988. "The Dynamics of Inclusion and Distance in Fieldwork Relations." In *Contemporary Fieldwork*, pp. 235-252, edited by R. Emerson. Prospect Hights. Ill.: Waveland Press.

Priestly, P. 1980. *Community of Scapegoats*. London: Pergamon Press.

Prus, R. 1975. "Resisting Designations: An Extension of Attribution Theory in a Negotiated Context." *Sociological Inquiry* 45, 3-14.

_____. 1982. "Designating Discretion and Openness: the Problematics of Truthfulness in Everyday Life." *Canadian Review of Sociology and Anthropology* 19, 70-91.

Pryce-Jones, D. 1977. "Not Their Finest Hour." *New Republic* May 14, vol. 177, 12.

Radzinowicz, L. 1956. *A History of English Criminal Law*. vol. 2. London: Stevens & Sons.

Reuter, P. 1983. "Licensing Criminals: Police and Informants." In *ABSCAM Ethics*, edited by G. Caplan. New York: Ballinger.

Richards, P. 1986. "Risk." in *Writing for Social Scientists*. pp. 108-120 Becker, H. Chicago: University of Chicago Press.

Richardson, L. 1988. "Secrecy and Status: The Social Construction of Forbidden Relationships." *American Sociological Review* 53, 209-219.

Rieber-Mohn, H. 1969. *Forrädere? - Streiflys over landssvikets problem*. Oslo: Aschehoug.

Rotenberg, M. 1974. "Self-Labelling. A Missing Link in the 'Societal Reaction' Theory of Deviance." *Sociological Review* 22, 335-354.

Rozovsky, L. E. and F. A. Rozovsky. 1981. "Public Health and the Law - Health Professionals as Police Informers." *Canadian Journal of Public Health* 27, 423-424.

Rubenstein, J. 1978. "Private Information." In *Policing: A View from the Street*, pp. 129-140, edited by P. Manning. Santa Monica, Calif.: Goodyear.

Runeberg, J. L. (1848, 1860) 1925. *The Songs of Ensign Stål*. (Fänrik Ståls sägner). Translated by Clement Burbank Shaw. New York: G. E. Stechert.

Schein, E. H., et al. 1957. "Distinguishing Characteristics of Collaborators and Resisters among American Prisons of War." *The Journal of Abnormal and Social Psychology* 55, 197-201.

Schein, E. H. 1971 *Coercive Persuasion*. New York: Norton.

Schillinger, E. 1988. "Dependency, Control, and Isolation: Battered Women and the Welfare System." *Journal of Contemporary Ethnography* 16, 469-490.

Schrag, C. 1944. *Social Types in a Prison Community*. Unpub. M.A. Thesis. Seattle: University of Washington.

Schrecker, E. W. 1986. *No Ivory Tower - McCarthyism & the Universities*. New York, Oxford: Oxford University Press.

Segal, J. 1957. "Correlates of Collaboration and Resistance Behavior Among U.S. Army POWs in Korea". *Journal of Social Issues* 13, 31-40.

Shibutani, T. 1966. *Improvised News - A Sociological Study of Rumor*. New York: Bobbs-Merrill.

Shils, E. A. 1956. *The Torment of Secrecy - the Background and Consequences of American Security Policies*. London: Heinemann.

Shover, N. 1971. *Burglary as an Occupation*. Ph. D. diss. Urbana: University of Illinois.

Simmel, G. (1908) 1955. *Conflict and the Webb of Group-Affiliations*. Trans. K. Wolff. New York: Free Press.

____. 1964. *The Sociology of Georg Simmel*. Trans., edited by K. Wolff. Part four, The Secret and the Secret Society. pp. 307-355. New York: Free Press.

Skagen, K. 1985. *Retten som ingen kunne målbinde - en forsvarstale for Arne Treholt*. Oslo: Ex Libris.

Skolnick, J. 1967. *Justice Without Trial*. New York: Wiley.

Smith, B. L. 1954. "English Treason Trials and Confessions in the 16th Century." *Journal of the History of Ideas* XV, 471-498.

Softley, P. 1980. "An Observational Study in Four Police Stations". In *Police Interrogation*. London: HMSO, Royal Commission on Criminal Procedure. Research studies no. 4.

SPANARKgruppen - narkotikaspaning och underrättelseförfarande. 1980. Stockholm: Rikspolisstyrelsen.

Stenross, B. and S. Kleinmann. 1988. "The Highs and Lows of Emotional Labor." *Journal of Contemporary Ethnography* 14, 435-452.

Stevenson's Book of Quotations - selected and arranged by Burton Stevenson. 1934. London: Cassell & Co.

Suttles, G. 1970. "Friendship as a Social Institution." In *Social Relationships*, edited by G. McCall. pp. 95-135. Chicago: Aldine.

Sykes, G. and D. Matza. 1957. "Techniques of Neutralization." *American Journal of Sociology* 22, 664-670.

Sylvester, S., et al. 1974. *Homocide in Prisons*. Unpubl. staff report, Washington, D.C.: National Institute of Law Enforcement and Criminal Justice.

Tamm, D. 1985. *Retsopgoret efter besaettelsen. Del 1 & 2*. Viborg: Jurist - og Ekonomforbundets Forlag.

Taylor, L. 1976. "Strategies for Coping with a Deviant Sentence." In *Life Sentences*, edited by R. Harré. London: Wiley.

Tennien, M. 1952. *No Secret is Safe -Behind the Bambo Curtain*. New York: Farrar, Straus and Young.

Thorne, B. 1979. "Political Activist as Participant Observer: Conflicts of Commitment in a Study of the Draft Resistance Movement of the 1960's." *Symbolic Interaction* 2, 73-88.

Tolan, S. and C. A. Bassett. 1985. "Operation Sojourner - Informers in the Sanctuary Movement." *The Nation* July 20/27, pp. 40-43.

Usborne, R. 1988. *The Penguin Wodehouse Companion*. London: Penguin.

Van Maanen, J. 1988. "The Moral Fix: On the Ethics of Fieldwork." In *Contemporary Fieldwork*, edited by R. Emerson, pp. 269-287. Prospect Heights: Waveland.

Vandivier, K. 1978. "Why Should my Conscience Bother Me?" In *Corporate and Governmental Deviance*, edited by M. D. Ermann and R. J. Lundman. New York: Oxford University Press.

Visser, G. 1976. *OB: Traitors or Patriots?* Johannesburg: Macmillan.

Vosper, C. 1971. *The Mind Benders*. London: Neville Spearman.

Waller, L. 1976. *Hide in Plain Sight*. New York: Delacorte Press.

Walzer, M. 1987. "Notes on Self-Criticism." *Social Research* 54, 33-43.

Ward, D. and G. Kassebaum. 1965. *Women in Prison*. Chicago: Aldine.

Ward, J. 1982. "Telling Tales in Prison." In *Custom and Conflict in British Society*, edited by R. Frankenberg. London: Manchester University Press.

Warren, C. 1986. "The Mental Patient as Betrayer." *Sociology of Health & Illness* 8, 233-251.

West, R. 1964. *The New Meaning of Treason*. New York: Viking.

———. 1970. *Violence and the Police - A Sociological Study of Law, Custom, and Morality.* Cambridge, Mass.: MIT Press.

Westley, W. 1956. "Secrecy and the Police." *Social Forces* 34, 254-257.

Whyte, W. F. 1973. *Street Corner Society.* Chicago: University of Chicago Press.

Wieder, L. D. 1974. *Language and Social Reality.* The Hauge/Paris: Mouton.

———. 1988. "Telling the Convict Code". In *Contemporary Fieldwork*, pp. 78-90, edited by R. Emerson. Prospect Heights, Ill.: Waveland Press.

Willis, P. 1977. *Learning to Labour.* Farnborough: Saxon House.

Wilmer, H. 1965. "The role of a 'rat' in prison." *Federal Probation* 29, 44-49.

Wright, P. 1987. *Spycatcher - the Candid Autobiography of a Senior Intelligence Officer.* New York: Viking.

Yngvesson, B. 1978. "The Reasonable Man and the Unreasonable Gossip." In *Essays in Memory of Max Gluckman*, pp. 133-154, edited by P. H. Gulliver. Leiden: E. J. Brill.

Znaniecki, F. 1952. *Cultural Sciences.* Urbana: University of Illinois Press.

Index